The ESSENT...

D0069633

ANCIENT HISTORY

— 4500 BC to 500 AD —
The Emergence of
Western Civilization

Gordon M. Patterson, Ph.D.
Associate Professor of History
Florida Institute of Technology
Melbourne, Florida

Research & Education Association
61 Ethel Road West
Piscataway, New Jersey 08854

THE ESSENTIALS®
OF ANCIENT HISTORY
4500 B.C. to 500 A.D.
The Emergence of Western Civilization

Printed in the United States of America

Library of Congress Catalog Card Number 97-76303

International Standard Book Number 0-87891-704-7

ESSENTIALS is a registered trademark of
Research & Education Association, Piscataway, New Jersey 08854

What the "Essentials of History" Will Do for You

REA's "Essentials of History" series offers a new approach to the study of history that is different from what has been available previously. Each book in the series has been designed to steer a sensible middle course, by including neither too much nor too little information.

Compared with conventional history outlines, the "Essentials of History" offer far more detail, with fuller explanations and interpretations of historical events and developments. Compared with voluminous historical tomes and textbooks, the "Essentials of History" offer a far more concise, less ponderous overview of each of the periods they cover.

The "Essentials of History" are intended primarily to aid students in studying history, doing homework, writing papers and preparing for exams. The books are organized to provide quick access to information and explanations of the important events, dates, and persons of the period. The books can be used in conjunction with any text. They will save hours of study and preparation time while providing a firm grasp and insightful understanding of the subject matter.

Instructors too will find the "Essentials of History" useful. The books can assist in reviewing or modifying course outlines. They also can assist with preparation of exams, as well as serve as an efficient memory refresher.

In sum, the "Essentials of History" will prove to be handy reference sources at all times.

The authors of the series are respected experts in their fields. They present clear, well-reasoned explanations and interpretations of the complex political, social, cultural, economic and philosophical issues and developments which characterize each era.

In preparing these books REA has made every effort to assure their accuracy and maximum usefulness. We are confident that each book will prove enjoyable and valuable to its user.

Dr. Max Fogiel, Program Director

CONTENTS

CHAPTER 1

THE EARLIEST BEGINNINGS OF CIVILIZATION

1.1 HISTORY AND PREHISTORY

1.1.1 *Definition of History*

The word "history" comes from the Greek "historia," which means "to inquire" or "to research." The content of history consists of all past human actions (thought and deed). Historians are responsible for discovering "facts" or "evidence" about past actions and interpreting or evaluating the meaning of these "facts" as they narrate the story of the past.

1.1.2 *Period of Ancient History*

Ancient history covers the period from the first appearance of human beings up to the middle of the sixth century of the Common Era (550 C.E.).

1.1.3 *Difference Between History and Prehistory*

Prehistory refers to the period prior to the discovery of writing around 3500 B.C.E. (Before the Common Era) in the ancient Near East. Before the discovery of writing, historians rely on the techniques of archaeologists and anthropologists in constructing their descriptions of ancient life.

1.2 THE APPEARANCE OF MAN

1.2.1 *Human Evolution*

Scientists estimate that the Earth is 4 to 6 billion years old. A controversy rages among paleontologists (scholars who study fossils and ancient forms of life) as to the date of the evolutionary split between ape-like (pongids) and man-like (hominid) creatures. A few scholars maintain that an animal called *Ramapithecus,* which lived 14 million years ago, is man's most distant ancestor. Most paleontologists, however, believe that the evolutionary split which led to the appearance of *Homo sapiens* (thinking man) occurred 4 million years ago. Fossil remains from East Africa of the earliest known hominid, *Australopithecus afarensis,* support this conclusion. Though this creature did not belong to the *Homo* family, one branch of its descendents developed a larger brain, a slender body, and smaller teeth, and is therefore considered the direct ancestor of modern humans.

1.2.2 *The First Humans*

In 1974, Donald Johanson and Maurice Taieb discovered in Ethiopia a partial skeleton of a three-foot-tall female member of the species *Australopithecus afarensis.* Known popularly as Lucy, she was very apelike in build and estimated to be just over 3 million years old. Emerging perhaps 2.5 million years ago was *Homo habilis,* who walked erect, had a larger brain than the apes, and fashioned primitive tools. In 1960, the first early member of this genus was identified by Louis Leakey at Olduvai Gorge in Tanzania. *Homo habilis* is the likely immediate ancestor to *Homo erectus* (who appeared about 1.6 mil-

2

lion years ago), which is to say, the first in a line that leads to us. It was Richard Leakey who, in 1984, found a nearly intact skeleton of *Homo erectus* that was more than 1.5 million years old; the fossil was dubbed Turkana Boy (after Lake Turkana in northern Kenya). Members of this species were taller than their predecessors and possessed a brain sufficiently developed to allow them to make stone tools and harness fire.

1.2.3 From Nature to History

Early human development was marked by four periods of glaciation (Ice Ages) that occurred intermittently from 3 million B.C.E. to 40,000 B.C.E. Humans (*Homo sapiens*) appeared near the beginning of the last Ice Age (80,000-70,000 B.C.E.). *Homo sapiens,* sometimes called Cro-Magnon Man (after a cave where fossil remains were discovered in France), shared the world with other populations. Neanderthal Man (whose remains were discovered in the Neander River valley in Germany) was Cro-Magnon Man's chief competitor. Neanderthals lived in camps, used fire, and ritualistically buried their dead. Cro-Magnon Man triumphed over his rivals by 40,000 B.C.E. (end of last Ice Age).

1.3   STAGES OF HUMAN HISTORY

1.3.1 Epochs of Human Development

The earliest ancestors of the human race left no written records. Archaeologists use the remains of prehistoric man's material culture (broken tools, artifacts, and burial sites) as the basis for their description of antiquity. All of history can be divided into two great periods: The Age of Stone and the Age of Metals. Each of these ages derives its character from the material that formed the basis of its development. The earliest tools were made of stone. Metal tools did not appear until 3500 B.C.E.

THE STAGES OF HUMAN DEVELOPMENT

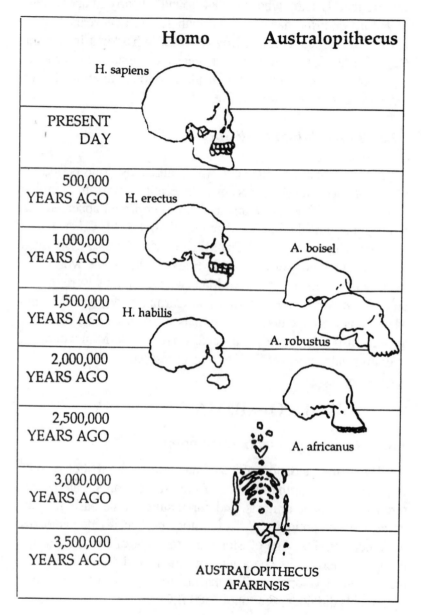

	Homo	Australopithecus
H. sapiens		
PRESENT DAY		
500,000 YEARS AGO	H. erectus	
1,000,000 YEARS AGO		A. boisel
1,500,000 YEARS AGO	H. habilis	
2,000,000 YEARS AGO		A. robustus
2,500,000 YEARS AGO		A. africanus
3,000,000 YEARS AGO		
3,500,000 YEARS AGO	AUSTRALOPITHECUS AFARENSIS	

1.4   THE PALEOLITHIC AGE

1.4.1   *The Early Paleolithic Age*

Archaeologists divide the Age of Stone into the Paleolithic Age (Old Stone Age) and the Neolithic Age (New Stone Age). The Paleolithic period runs from roughly 2 million B.C.E. to 10,000 B.C.E. The early Paleolithic peoples (up to 30,000 B.C.E.) lived as foragers. Hunting and gathering formed the basis of human life. The availability of food regulated population growth. Humans lived in small groups of 20 to 50 members. Archaeological evidence suggests that the earliest division of labor was based on gender.

1.4.2   *The Later Paleolithic Age*

Between 30,000 and 10,000 B.C.E., Paleolithic peoples showed a notable advance. New and more complicated tools like the fish-hook and harpoon appeared. Animal skins were sewn (the needle was invented during this period) into garments and caves were used for shelter. But perhaps the most remarkable legacy from the late Paleolithic Age are the extraordinarily naturalistic depictions of bison, bulls, fish, and other creatures that appear on the walls and ceilings of caves (25,000 B.C.E.). The motivation for these paintings was probably a desire to create some kind of sympathetic magic that would ensure the supply of animals for the clan (an extended family) or tribe (a group of clans).

1.4.3   *End of Paleolithic Age*

The Old Stone Age ended around 10,000. The retreat of the glaciers that followed the end of the Ice Age transformed the available food supply. Some animals, such as the reindeer, migrated to the north. Others, such as the mammoth, became extinct. The period from 10,000 to 5000 is called the Mesolithic Age (Middle Stone Age). This was a transitional period in which new sources of food supply were developed and humans assumed a more sedentary existence. The beginning and end of the Mesolithic Age varied. Some peoples had entered into a new productive relationship with nature by 10,000 B.C.E.

1.5   THE NEOLITHIC AGE

1.5.1   *The Agricultural Revolution*

The development of systematic agriculture and the domestication of animals (10,000 to 6000 B.C.E. in the Near East) made possible the emergence of civilization. Wheat and barley were probably the first wild grasses to come under cultivation. Animals such as sheep, goats, pigs, and donkeys were adapted to human use. Archaeologists speculate that the dog was the

LAND RESOURCES

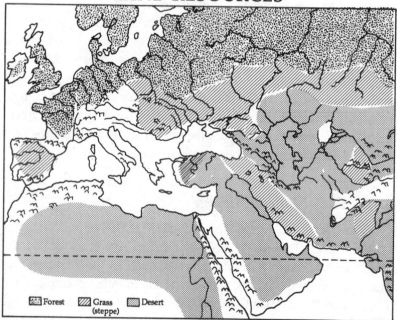

Forest   Grass (steppe)   Desert

first animal to become domesticated. Systematic agriculture and the domestication of animals gave humans control over their food supply.

1.5.2 Economic and Social Character of Neolithic Cultures

The agricultural revolution provoked changes in population, the division of labor, and trade.

Population. The revolution in agriculture had a direct impact on population growth. Archaeologists have found evidence of a sharp increase in population among Neolithic peoples. Population size was limited in the Paleolithic Age by the food resources of a given territory. Agriculture removed this restriction. Children become economically useful as agricultural workers whereas in the Paleolithic Age children posed a burden to the clan or tribe's movement. After 8000 B.C.E., villages appeared in such places as Jericho (Palestine), Jarma (Iraq/Kurdistan), and Catal Huyuk (western Turkey).

Division of Labor. The division of labor became more complex in the Neolithic Age. The existence of an agricultural surplus permitted specialization. There is evidence that women were the first farmers. They used crude hoes to cultivate small patches of land. The discovery of the plow and the domestication of oxen probably changed this, creating new work for men. The settled life of Neolithic villages facilitated the establishment of traditions, crafts, and lasting institutions.

Trade. The agricultural revolution marked the beginning of commerce between different regions. Different Neolithic peoples traded with one another, exchanging raw materials and handcrafts.

1.5.3 Neolithic Culture and Technological Innovations

Neolithic culture spread to every part of the habitable world.

Despite their many differences, Neolithic cultures possess certain common traits such as woodworking, pottery manufacture, and a textile industry.

Woodworking. During the Paleolithic Age tools were manufactured from stone by one of two processes: chipping flakes (Flake Cultures) or cutting away from a core (Core Cultures). In the Neolithic period, tools with edges that had been ground down appeared for the first time. These improved stone tools were used for grinding grain and/or attached to pieces of wood to form hoes and plows. These improved tools facilitated the use of wood.

Pottery. Pottery probably emerged out of the need for vessels in the preparation and storage of foods. The discovery of pottery is one of the earliest examples of early man's efforts to control and utilize the processes of chemical change. "Firing" transforms clay's consistency and color.

Textiles. Knitting and weaving were developed by Neolithic peoples. Spinning wool appeared shortly after the domestication of animals. Cotton was cultivated as early as 3000 B.C.E. in the Indus Valley.

1.6   THE APPEARANCE OF CIVILIZATION

Between 4000 and 3000 B.C.E., the earliest civilizations appeared in the Near East. Between 6000 and 3000 B.C.E., humans invented the plow, utilized the wheel, harnessed the wind, discovered how to smelt copper ores, and began to develop accurate solar calendars. These events were part of a gradual process in which small villages grew into populous cities. Civilization begins with the appearance of the first cities.

1.6.1   *Definition of Culture and Civilization*

The word "culture" refers to the variety of ways of living

EARLY HUMAN SETTLEMENTS

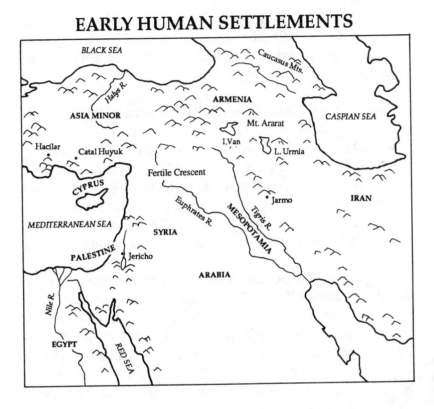

(thought and action) created by a group and transmitted to its successors. Paleolithic and Neolithic cultures depended on an oral tradition to transmit the skills and discoveries of one generation to the next. The invention of writing (3500 B.C.E., in Mesopotamia) marks the beginning of civilization and divides prehistoric from historic times.

1.6.2 *Causes for the Rise of Civilization*

A number of theories seek to account for the appearance of civilization after 4000 B.C.E. Climate, geography, economic resources, food supply, and cross-cultural contact have been offered as explanations for the rise of specific civilizations.

Climate and Geography. The most popular explanation for the rise of civilization links climate and geography. Philosophers such as Aristotle and Montaigne advocated this interpretation.

Soil Exhaustion Theory. Modern conservationists argue that civilization is tied to the problem of soil exhaustion. Neolithic farmers constantly faced the inevitability of overworking the land. They faced the choice of either moving periodically or of finding a way to renew the soil. Proponents of the soil exhaustion theory point to the rise of civilization in river valleys as evidence for their position. The flooding of a river revitalizes the soil, making continued farming possible.

Toynbee's Theory of Challenge and Response. Arnold Toynbee (1889-1975), the British historian, believed that civilization rose out of a series of challenges that confronted human beings. Each of these challenges provoked a response that either brought the advance of civilization or marked a setback. Toynbee's challenges include natural conditions like drought and topography as well as challenges man creates for himself, such as war and slavery.

1.6.3 *The First Civilizations*

Archaeologists and historians disagree as to which of the great civilizations of antiquity was the oldest. Some scholars believe that the first civilization appeared in the Nile Valley in Egypt. More think that civilization first appeared in the area between the Tigris and Euphrates Rivers in Mesopotamia. In both ancient Egypt and Mesopotamia the transformation of scattered sedentary villages into urban civilizations was facilitated by the availability of water supply, the need for collective action in the building of dikes and reservoirs, and the enlargement of the farmer's diet, which followed the introduction of fruit, date, and olive trees during this period.

THE EARLIEST BEGINNINGS
OF CIVILIZATION
(All dates are approximate B.C.E.)

Ramapithecus	14,000,000	B.C.E.
Australopithecus afarensis		
(*Africanus*)	4,000,000	
Homo habilis	3,500,000	
Glacial Age	3,000,000	- 10,000
First (Guenz) glaciation	3,000,000	
Homo erectus	2,000,000	
Second (Mindel) glaciation	800,000	
Third (Riss) glaciation	265,000	
Neanderthal man flourished	86,000	- 40,000
Fourth (Wuerm) glaciation	75,000	
Homo sapiens	before 70,000	
Great period of Paleolithic Art	30,000	- 17,000
The Forest Folk	14,000	- 8000
Paleolithic period ends	10,000	
Mesolithic period in the Near East	10,000	- 7000
The first villages	7000	
Neolithic period in the Near East	7000	
Use of metals	5000	
Swiss Lake Villages	4500	- 2500
Megaliths	3500	- 2000
Civilization begins	before 3000	
Writing	before 3000	
Bronze Age in the Near East	before 3000	
Iron Age in the Near East	before 1000	

CHAPTER 2

MESOPOTAMIAN CIVILIZATION

2.1 GEOGRAPHY AND CLIMATE

2.1.1 *Geography*

The character of Mesopotamian civilization was determined in large part by geography and climate. Mesopotamia refers to the 600-mile-long alluvial valley between the Tigris and Euphrates rivers. The region's boundaries were the Taurus Mountains in the North, the Zagros Mountains in the East, the Syrian and Arabian Deserts in the West, and the Persian Gulf in the South. Mesopotamia was one part of the Fertile Crescent, which rises out of the Persian Gulf, curving across northern Syria and down through Palestine to Egypt. The major civilizations of the Near East appeared within these geographical limits.

2.1.2 *Environmental Challenges*

The climate and geography of Mesopotamia were inhospitable and unproductive. Droughts alternated with periods of flooding and violent storms. All of the Mesopotamian peoples

12

were confronted with the problems of flooding and increasing salinization.

Flooding. The Tigris and Euphrates rivers originate in different mountain ranges. Usually, flooding occurs in the spring as snow melts in the mountains. The flatness of the alluvial plain and vagaries of winter storms in the Taurus and Zagros mountains made flooding a constant threat in Mesopotamia. This compelled early Mesopotamian cultures to undertake collective actions like the building of dikes, digging of reservoirs, and construction of irrigation ditches.

Salinization. The success of Mesopotamian city-states in building canals and irrigation systems added to the existing problem of salinization. As the land was irrigated, salt leached (wicked) upward, making the soil useless. Salinization forced the different Mesopotamian city-states into a competition for arable land. Since Mesopotamia possessed no natural frontiers, this contributed to the near-constant state of warfare that existed throughout antiquity in Mesopotamia.

2.2   STAGES OF DEVELOPMENT OF MESOPOTAMIAN CIVILIZATION

2.2.1   *Sumer* (4000 to 2300 B.C.E.)

The earliest Mesopotamian civilization emerged in the southern part of the alluvial plain in the Valley of Sumer (Shinar) around 3500 B.C.E. The origin of the Sumerians is uncertain. Their language is unlike any other in the region. The Sumerians described their origin as lying in the East "where the sun rises." The principal Sumerian city-states were Ur, Lagash, Eridu, and Uruk. The *Gilgamesh*, a long epic poem written around 2000 B.C.E., expressed the Sumerian conception of the relation of man and the gods.

EARLY MESOPOTAMIA

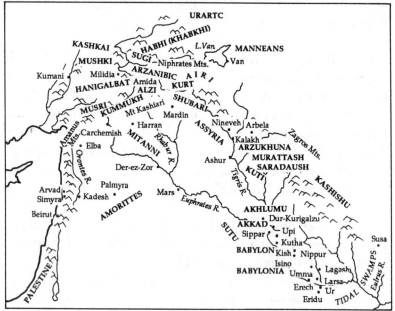

2.2.2 *Akkad* (2300 to 2200 B.C.E.)

The Akkadians were a Semitic people who occupied the Sumerian city-states after 2400 B.C.E. In 2340 B.C.E. the Akkadian king Sargon proclaimed himself a "world conqueror." The Akkadian language replaced Sumerian. The Akkadians adopted the Sumerian culture. Between 2200 and 2000 B.C.E. there was a Sumerian revival in which the Akkadians and Sumerians became indistinguishable.

2.2.3 *Amor* (Old Babylonians 2000 to 1550 B.C.E.)

The Amorites overwhelmed their rivals by 1900 B.C.E. They established a new capital city at Babylon. The capital's Hanging Gardens were recognized in antiquity as one of the Seven Wonders of the World. The Amorites are known as the Old Babylonians. They preserved much of the Sumerian tradition.

The sixth Amorite king, Hammurabi (1792-1750 B.C.E.), promulgated a legal code which unified the entire lower Tigris-Euphrates Valley.

2.2.4 Hittites and Kassites

Old Babylon fell (approximately 1595 B.C.E.) to bands of Hittite raiders from Asia Minor (modern Turkey). The Hittites withdrew, leaving Mesopotamia to the Kassites. The Kassites ruled Mesopotamia until 1000 B.C.E.

2.2.5 The Assyrians (1100-612 B.C.E.)

The Assyrians were a fierce, warlike people who originated in Asia Minor. By 665 B.C.E., Assyrian warriors had conquered Syria and Palestine and much of Mesopotamia. Their southern border was Egypt. The Assyrians used terror to govern subject peoples. Their soldiers were among the first to carry weapons made of iron.

2.2.6 The Chaldeans (New Babylonians 612-538 B.C.E.)

The Chaldeans drove the Assyrians out of the lower Tigris-Euphrates Valley in 612 B.C.E. In 587 B.C.E. the Chaldeans conquered Syria and Palestine. Their king, Nebuchadnezzar, destroyed the Temple of Solomon and ordered that the leading Jews in Jerusalem should be brought to Babylon as slaves (Babylonian Captivity in the Book of Daniel). Cyrus, King of the Medes and Persians, defeated the Chaldeans in 538 B.C.E.

2.2.7 The Persians

Little is known of the Persians prior to their victory over the Chaldeans. Initially they were the vassals of the Medes (a people who controlled the area that was north and east of the Tigris River). Cyrus, king of the southern Persians, led his satrapies (vassals) in a successful campaign against the Medes in 559 B.C.E. In the next twenty years his armies created a vast empire. In 539 B.C.E., Cyrus conquered the Chaldeans. Cambyses, Cyrus's son, conquered Egypt in 525 B.C.E. Cambyses's successor was Darius the Great. Darius governed between 522 and 486 B.C.E. He extended the Persian Empire, bringing the Persians into conflict with the Greeks. Xerxes, Darius's successor, failed in his attempt to conquer the Greeks in 479 B.C.E. The Persians constructed a network of roads which provided a communications system for the government. The Royal Road ran for more than 1600 miles from Susa (on the Persian Gulf) to Sardis (in Asia Minor).

2.3 POLITICAL AND SOCIAL HISTORY

2.3.1 *The Sumerian Paradigm*

The Sumerians established the pattern for civilization in Mesopotamia. They were the first to respond to the twin problems of flooding and salinization. They constructed dikes and built reservoirs and formed a loose confederation between their city-states. Typically, city-states covered an area of approximately 100 square miles. The city-states were independent and joined together under a common leader (patesi) when confronted with an external threat. The Sumerian confederation of city-states was unable to withstand the influx of Semitic peoples. Sargon (ca. 2350) made himself king of a "universal dominion."

2.3.2 *The Babylonian Empire*

The Amorite victory over the Akkadians (ca. 2000 B.C.E.) catalyzed a series of important political and cultural developments. Through trade, the Babylonians influenced much of the ancient world. The Code of Hammurabi (ca. 1750) elaborated a way of life that had developed for centuries. The Code presents a compilation of traditions and laws that were shared by many of the Mesopotamian peoples. The Code of Hammurabi has a number of distinctive features:

1) The administration of justice is unequal. Membership in a social class determines the punishment for a crime. In Old Babylon there were three classes. The highest class consisted of the King, his retinue, priests, and wealthy individuals. The second class was made up of free individuals. Slaves belonged to the lowest class.

2) The idea of justice was based on a concept of retribution or *lex talionis* (law of reciprocal punishment in kind — "an eye for an eye").

3) The administration of justice was semi-private. Individuals and families bore much of the responsibility for enforcing the Code.

2.3.3 *Government*

Recent archaeological research has called into question the long-held belief that the Babylonian government was a theocracy (government by priests). Priests controlled a substantial amount of property but individual owners predominated. The King (lugal) exercised power independently from the temple.

2.3.4 *The Assyrian Empire*

The Assyrian political development was unlike that of any of the other Mesopotamian peoples. Their relative isolation until 1300 B.C.E. and the necessities of waging constant warfare after this date led them to develop an extremely militaristic system. The Assyrians disseminated stories of their cruelty and brutality in order to terrorize their subject peoples. Archaeologists disagree on how much influence the Sumerians and Old Babylonians had on the Assyrians. Some parts of the Code of Hammurabi were maintained. Significant changes were made in the lex talionis and the Babylonian system of punishment which was based on social class. Finally, where the Babylonians reserved the most severe penalties for treason, the Assyri-

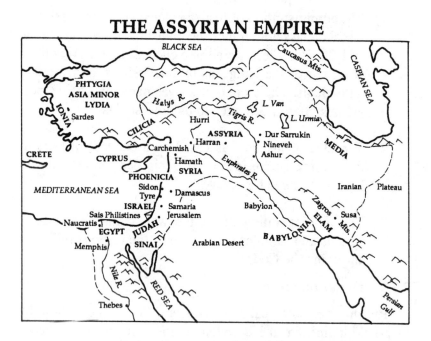

THE ASSYRIAN EMPIRE

ans prescribed the greatest penalties for homosexuality and abortion. Some contend that the reason the Assyrians considered these acts so grave was because they might lead to a lower birthrate and adversely affect the size of the military.

2.4 SCIENCE AND TECHNOLOGY IN MESOPOTAMIA

2.4.1 *The Invention of Writing*

There is some evidence that writing may have been invented as early as 9000 B.C.E. Most historians credit the Sumerians with beginning the tradition of writing that runs to the present. The earliest Sumerian writing (3500 B.C.E.) consisted of inscriptions on clay tablets and cylinders. This writing is called *cuneiform* because of its wedge-like character (the Latin word "cuneus" means "wedge"). A reed stylus was used to make impressions on clay tablets about the size of an adult's hand.

2.4.2   Stages in the Development of Writing

Writing developed in at least three stages:

1) *Pictographs.* The earliest form of writing, the thing being depicted is represented by a picture.

2) *Ideograms.* A sign or symbol is used to represent a class of things.

3) *Phonogram.* A sign or symbol represents a specific sound. The Phoenicians (people who lived in what is now Lebanon) are credited with spreading the use of the modern alphabet (after 1900 B.C.E.), the origin of which is unknown. The Greeks adopted the alphabet from Phoenician traders in the eighth century. The Greeks in turn passed this alphabet to the Romans, who made minor changes in it.

2.4.3   Mathematics

The Sumerians contributed much to the development of mathematics. By 2500 B.C.E. their mathematicians devised multiplication tables for their sexagesimal numerical system. Surviving mathematical records demonstrate that the Sumerians utilized a system of place notation and had discovered a general solution for quadratic equations. Later the Assyrians applied the Sumerian sexagesimal system to geometry and divided the circle into 360 degrees.

2.4.4   Astronomy

Records of astronomical observations in Mesopotamia can be traced to before 2000 B.C.E. After 700 B.C.E., observations were accurate and systematically tabulated. These records allowed the Mesopotamians to identify the Saronic cycle (lunar eclipses occurring every eighteen years). Sometime after 2000 B.C.E. the Mesopotamians divided the year into twelve months with 30 days each. They divided the week into seven days (one day for each of the celestial bodies) and the day into twenty-four hours based on sexagesimal minutes and seconds. Finally, the Babylonians created a stellar map that described the twelve constellations (one for each month) in the equatorial belt through which the sun passes (the zodiac).

2.5   RELIGION

2.5.1   *Sumerian*

The *Gilgamesh Epic* (poem composed ca. 2000 B.C.E. which contains an account of the biblical flood) presents the religious outlook of the Sumerian and subsequent Mesopotamian peoples. The gods were divided into warring factions that struggled for control of the Earth. The poem centers on the unsuccessful effort of the protagonist (a quasi-legendary King who lived ca. 2800 B.C.E.) to escape death. Archaeologists have discovered numerous clay tablets that describe the rituals, prayers, magical incantations, and procedures used to learn the will of the gods (divination) that the Babylonians employed. The focal point of religious practices was in the temple that stood atop the city's ziggurat (stepped mound).

2.5.2   *The Chaldean Religion*

The Chaldeans tried to revive the Old Babylonian precepts. They restored Marduk as the chief of the gods. In fact, the Chaldeans practiced an essentially astral religion. The gods were envisioned as forces beyond human understanding which were centered in the heavenly bodies. Chief among the Chaldean beliefs was the necessity of submitting to fate. Surviving texts and temple ornaments indicate that the Chaldeans were uninterested in questions about life after death.

2.5.3 The Persian Religion

Zoroastrianism was the Persian religion. The prophet Zoroaster established the essentials of this religion shortly before 600 B.C.E. Zoroastrianism is known primarily as a monotheistic religion characterized by worship of the holy god Ahura Mazda, who seeks to enlist the goodness of humankind in his cosmic struggle against the evil spirit Ahriman. After death, humans are rewarded or punished on the basis of how responsibly they conduct their lives. Those who sin are sentenced to a period of retribution in hell. Unlike in Christianity, however, all Zoroastrians eventually do find a place in heaven.

2.6 REASONS FOR DECLINE

A near-constant state of warfare existed in Mesopotamia. This prevented any city-state or group of city-states from developing enough power to hold off its rivals. After 538 B.C.E., Mesopotamia came under the rule of a succession of empires and dynasties.

2.6.1 The Contributions of Mesopotamia to Civilization

The civilization of the Mesopotamian peoples exercised an influence far beyond the boundaries of the Tigris and Euphrates rivers. Traders carried the Sumerian lunar calendar, use of the wheel, and a system of weights and measures to the Mediterranean. The Etruscans in Italy (ca. 1000 B.C.E.) were influenced by the Sumerian system of divination. Babylonian architects pioneered the use of the arch and column later adopted by the Romans.

CHRONOLOGY OF THE MESOPOTAMIAN PEOPLES
(All dates are approximate B.C.E.)

Early Sumerian Settlements	3500 - 3200
Writing	before 3500
Royal Cemetery, First Dynasty Ur	2700
Sargon the Great of Akkad	2340
Amorite Invasion (Old Babylonians)	2000
Gilgamesh composed	2000
Hammurabi's reign	1792 - 1750
Hittites conquer Amorites and retreat to Asia Minor	1595
Kassites control Mesopotamia	1500 - 1000
Hittite Empire is destroyed	ca. 1200
Assyrian Empire	1100 - 612
Assyrian conquest of Mesopotamia	665
Chaldean Empire	612 - 538
Nebuchadnezzar destroys Jerusalem and brings Jews to Babylon	586
Persians defeat Chaldeans	539

Sumerian Period: *The White Temple*, 3500-3000 B.C.E. Warka.

CHAPTER 3

EGYPTIAN CIVILIZATION

3.1 GEOGRAPHY AND CLIMATE

Geography and climate account for much of Egypt's stability in the course of 3000 years of ancient history. Herodotus, the Greek historian of the fifth century B.C.E., identified the determinant role that geography played in the region's history when he described Egypt as "the gift of the Nile." Rising 4000 miles to the south in Central Africa, the Nile runs its course northwards to the Mediterranean. Rapids (called Cataracts) make the river impassible at six points. The northernmost of these rapids (the First Cataract) lies 750 miles from the sea at Syrene (Aswan). This point marked the northern boundary of Upper Egypt, which ran six hundred miles to the south. Lower Egypt consisted of the final 150 miles of the river's course. In Lower Egypt the Nile breaks into channels resembling a triangle (called the Delta because of its similarity to the Greek letter "delta").

3.1.1 Contrast with Mesopotamia

Egypt offers a sharp contrast to the inhospitable conditions present in Mesopotamia. The Nile does not flood erratically like the Tigris and Euphrates rivers. Additionally, the soil is

ANCIENT EGYPT

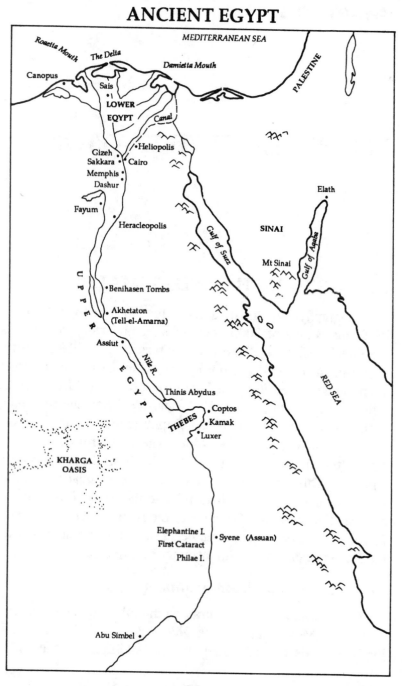

richer in the Nile valley, allowing two crops a year. Finally, whereas Mesopotamia possesses no natural barriers sufficiently formidable to invaders, Egypt is separated from potential adversaries by deserts in the west and east, equatorial jungles in the south, and the Mediterranean in the north.

3.2   OUTLINE OF EGYPTIAN HISTORY

Egyptian history divides into seven periods:

Archaic Period	5000 - 2685	B.C.E.
Old Kingdom	2685 - 2180	B.C.E.
First Intermediate Period	2180 - 2040	B.C.E.
Middle Kingdom	2040 - 1785	B.C.E.
Second Intermediate Period	1785 - 1560	B.C.E.
New Kingdom	1560 - 1085	B.C.E.
Post-Empire	1085 - 30	B.C.E.

3.2.1   *Archaic Period* (5000-2685 B.C.E.)

By 5000 B.C.E. prehistoric Egyptians had passed into the Neolithic Age. Agriculture was well-developed and copper was used to make tools. Sometime prior to 3000 B.C.E. the Egyptians invented a system of writing. Researchers believe that the Egyptian "hieroglyphs" (Greek for "sacred carvings") were influenced by the Mesopotamians. There were more than 40 large settlements along the Nile's course by 3000 B.C.E. Traditionally, Narmer or Menes is credited with unifying Upper and Lower Egypt. He is considered the first Pharaoh ("Great House"). The term *pharaoh* was not used by the Egyptians. This expression came into general usage because of the Bible.

3.2.2   *The Old Kingdom* (2685-2180 B.C.E.)

The Old Kingdom consisted of the first six dynasties of Egyptian rulers. During this period most of the traditions that were to become characteristic of Egyptian life for the next two thousand years appeared. The king was considered a living god and held absolute power. During the Third Dynasty (ca. 2650 B.C.E.) the capital was moved to Memphis, just north of the beginning of the Delta. The pyramids were built during the Fourth Dynasty (ca. 2613-2494 B.C.E.).

3.2.3 The First Intermediate Period (2180-2040 B.C.E.)

There are at least three reasons which account for the collapse of central government in the Old Kingdom. First, the expenditures necessary for projects such as the pyramids exhausted the state's revenues. Second, climatic disasters reduced the amount of grain, weakening the state. Finally, the nobility grew powerful and autonomous. During the First Intermediate Period, power reverted to the *nomes* (regional authorities).

3.2.4 The Middle Kingdom (2040-1785 B.C.E.)

This period of disorder and anarchy ended when a powerful noble family from Thebes subdued their rivals and established a new dynasty (ca. 2040 B.C.E.) The Middle Kingdom was one of brilliance. During the Twelfth Dynasty the Pharaohs undertook a massive land reclamation project at an oasis west of the Nile (The Fayum). Dams and reservoirs were constructed to insure adequate water supply throughout the year. The Thirteenth Dynasty (ca. 1785 B.C.E.), already weakened by a resurgence of the nobility, fell victim to external invaders.

3.2.5 The Second Intermediate Period (1785-1560 B.C.E.)

The invasion of Egypt by the Hyksos ("Rulers of Foreign Lands") marks a turning point in Egyptian history. Until 1700 B.C.E., Egypt had seemed impregnable. It is uncertain precisely what the origin of the Hyksos was. They brought three innovations: use of horses, chariots, and body armor. The Hyksos attempted to establish themselves as the rulers of Egypt. By

1560 they had either been driven out of Egypt or were enslaved.

3.2.6 *The New Kingdom* (1560-1085 B.C.E.)

The Hyksos invasion left a lasting impression on Egypt. The Egyptian sense of stability and security was shattered. Under the New Kingdom the Pharaohs followed a policy of expansion that saw them dominate Nubia in the south and send their armies into Palestine and Syria. Two new classes came into being: professional soldiers and slaves. It was during this period that the Jews fell under the Pharaoh's power. The Egyptian Empire reached its zenith by 1400 B.C.E. The Empire endured for four centuries. By 1085 B.C.E. the Egyptians had lost their Asian empire. Economic disasters ensued and the New Kingdom collapsed with the end of the Twentieth Dynasty.

3.2.7 *Post-Empire* (1085-30 B.C.E.)

Egypt was repeatedly invaded between 1085 and 30 B.C.E. The barbaric Libyans and Nubians were the first to attack. Between 663 and 525 B.C.E., Egypt was part of the Assyrian Empire. The Persians controlled Egypt between 525 and 325 B.C.E. Alexander the Great's armies conquered Egypt in 325 and made it part of his Empire. In 30 B.C.E. the Romans succeeded in bringing Egypt under their control.

3.3 POLITICAL AND SOCIAL CHARACTER OF EGYPTIAN LIFE

The pattern of Egyptian government was established in the Old Kingdom.

3.3.1 *Ma'at*

The Pharaoh possessed complete authority. The king ruled

as a living god. His chief responsibility was to rule according to "Ma'at." Ma'at is an Egyptian concept that includes justice, right, truth, law, and order.

3.3.2 *Social Classes*

There were four classes in the Old and Middle Kingdoms: the royal family, nobles, middle class (including scribes, artisans and wealthy farmers), and the peasants. Throughout the Old and Middle Kingdoms the peasants made up the great majority of the population. The invasion of the Hyksos added two new classes: professional soldiers and slaves. Agriculture was the basis of economic life. The gap between the rich and the poor was tremendous. Family life was built on monogamous marriage though polygamy was permitted. Women could own property and the Egyptians were one of the few ancient peoples that allowed women to succeed to the throne (Queen Hatshepsut in the Eighteenth Dynasty).

3.4 RELIGION

The Egyptian conception of religion was polytheistic. During the Archaic Period animism was widespread. Each village had its own pantheon of gods and spirits. The unification of Upper and Lower Egypt introduced a new stage in the evolution of Egyptian religious thought. In the Old Kingdom the Sun God, Re, emerged as the most powerful of the gods.

3.4.1 *Belief in an Afterlife*

The Egyptians were unique among ancient peoples in the emphasis they placed on life after death. Initially, they believed that the Pharaoh was the only person who was granted immortality. They conceived of death as an extension of life. This accounts for the elaborate preparations that culminated in the building of the pyramids. The Egyptians believed that it was

28

possible to preserve the Pharaoh's "ka" (vital spirit). The first pyramid (Step Pyramid) was designed by the architect and engineer Imhotep as the Pharaoh's stairway to heaven. In the Old Kingdom only the Pharaoh was granted immortality. In the Middle Kingdom the belief had grown to include everyone.

3.4.2 Osiris

During the Middle Kingdom Osiris, god of the underworld, attracted a wide following. Osiris was a vegetative god associated with the Nile. His followers believed that he had been murdered by his envious brother Seth. Seth killed Osiris because he coveted Isis, who was Osiris' sister/wife. Seth cut Osiris into pieces and threw them into the Nile in Upper Egypt. Horus, Osiris' dutiful son, collected the parts when they reached the Delta. Followers of the cult believed that Osiris was miraculously rejuvenated. His death and resurrection was taken as a guarantee of the possibility of an afterlife. The Osiris cult carried an ethical note. Funerary paintings from this period show the souls ("ka") being judged on the basis of how much good and evil the individual had done in his life.

3.4.3 Monotheism

The greatest innovation in the Egyptian conception of religion came in the New Kingdom during the reign of Amenhotep (1363-1347 B.C.E.). Amenhotep ("Amon rests") revolutionized Egyptian religious practices. He introduced the idea that there was a single god: Aton. He changed his name to Akhenaton ("Aton is satisfied") and commanded that the temples for the other gods be closed. Akhenaton moved his capital to El-Amarna, midway between Memphis and Thebes. The people did not worship Aton directly. They were instructed to worship Akhenaton as a living god who in turn worshipped Aton. Akhenaton's intolerance of the existing temples provoked a strong reaction. His successor, the boy king Tutankhaton, changed his name to Tutankhamen shortly after his predecessor's death. The name change signaled the return to the worship of Amon and the pantheon of Egyptian gods.

3.5 SCIENCE AND TECHNOLOGY

3.5.1 *Mathematics*

The Egyptians made fewer advances in mathematics than the Babylonians. They derived a better value for "pi" than the Babylonians but were unable to solve more than simple linear equations. Their number system was hampered because they possessed no notion of place-value.

3.5.2 *Astronomy*

There are no surviving records of systematic observations by the Egyptians that are comparable to the records kept by the Babylonians. Funerary paintings show that they divided the heavens into thirty-six constellations. The Egyptians devised a more accurate calendar than the Babylonians. They set the length of the year at 365 days based on twelve months with thirty days for each month. They added five intercalary days at the end of the year so as to keep the calendar tied to the solar year.

3.5.3 *Medicine*

In medicine the Egyptians produced notable advances. Medical papyri go back to 2000 B.C.E. These early texts present a "demon" theory of sickness. The disease is represented as being caused by an evil spirit. By 1600 B.C.E. medical texts reveal a considerable advance. The Edwin Smith Papyrus describes several dozen medical cases in detail. The physician makes a diagnosis, proposes a course of treatment, and makes a prognosis as to the probable outcome. Disease is treated as a purely natural phenomenon.

3.6 CONTRIBUTIONS OF EGYPT

Egyptian civilization bequeathed the idea of stability to subsequent civilizations. Practically, innovations like the invention of papyrus (a reed that was pressed together to form paper) insured that the records of the Egyptians would survive for future civilizations. The Egyptian belief in an afterlife and the funerary cult which developed around it were unique in the ancient world. The Egyptian conception of monotheism was short-lived and was never adopted by the people. The Hebrews, meanwhile, developed the idea of monotheism concurrently and, in contrast to the Egyptians, embraced it as the central tenet of their beliefs.

CHRONOLOGY OF EGYPTIAN HISTORY
(All dates are B.C.E. and approximate)

Dynasties I-II	3100	- 2685
Writing	before 3000	
Old Kingdom (Dynasties III-VI)	2685	- 2180
Pyramids of Khufu, Khafre, Menkaure		
(Fourth Dynasty)	2613	- 2494
First Intermediate Period	2180	- 2040
Middle Kingdom (Dynasties VIII-X)	2040	- 1785
Second Intermediate Period	1785	- 1560
Hyksos invasion	1674	
New Kingdom or Empire		
(Dynasties XVIII-XX)	1560	- 1085
Hashepsut	1490	- 1469
Amenhotep III	1402	- 1363
Akhenaten	1363	- 1347 ?
Ramses II	1298	- 1232
Battle of Kadesh	1287	

Ramses III	1198	- 1167
Egypt Conquered by Esarhaddon, king of Assyria	671	
Saite Period (Dynasty XXVI)	663	- 525
Egypt conquered by Cambyses, king of Persia	525	
Egypt conquered by Alexander the Great	332	
Egypt annexed by Rome	30	

Archaic Period, Dynasties I-III: *Step Pyramid*, Imhotep, 2650 B.C.E. Cut stone. Saqqara, Egypt.

Old Kingdom, Dynasties III-VI: *Pyramids of Menkaure, Khafre, and Khufu.* Pyramids, of which Khufu's was the largest, were started by him circa 2600 B.C.E. at Giza.

CHAPTER 4

THE HEBREW CIVILIZATION

4.1 ORIGIN OF THE HEBREW PEOPLE

4.1.1 *Geography*

Palestine and Syria constitute the narrow (ca. 100 miles wide) coastal plain that runs from the Taurus Mountains in north Asia Minor to the beginning of the Sinai Desert 400 miles to the south. The land generally experiences a mild Mediterranean climate with regular seasonal rainfall, and must certainly have seemed a "land flowing with milk and honey" to the nomadic Hebrews. The name "Palestine" derives from the seafaring people, the Peleset (Philistines), who were driven out of Egypt in the twelfth century by Ramses III.

4.1.2 *The Earliest Inhabitants*

The early history of Palestine is obscure. It is likely that the first people to settle in Palestine were part of the Semitic semi-nomadic tribes that occupied northern Mesopotamia. These tribes were related to the Amorites that occupied Mesopotamia about 2000 B.C.E. The Phoenicians and Aramaeans were among the first to inhabit the coastal plain.

PALESTINE AND THE MIDDLE EAST

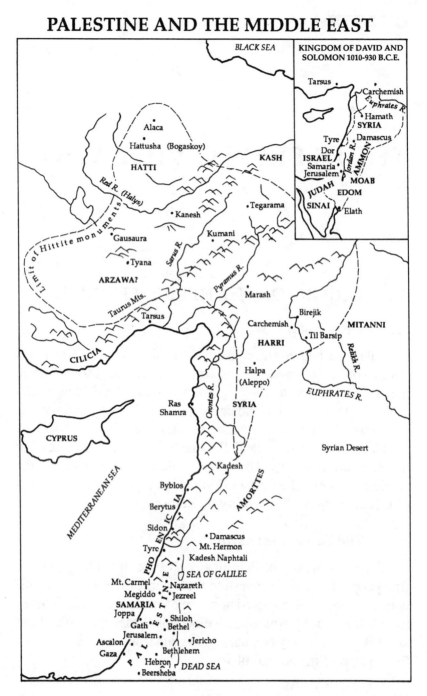

BLACK SEA

KINGDOM OF DAVID AND SOLOMON 1010-930 B.C.E.

Tarsus

Carchemish

Euphrates R.

Hamath

SYRIA

Tyre · Damascus

Dor

ISRAEL

Samaria · *Jordan R.*

Jerusalem

AMMON

MOAB

JUDAH

EDOM

SINAI

Elath

Alaca

Hattusha (Bogaskoy)

HATTI

KASH

Red R. (Halys)

Kanesh

· Tegarama

Limit of Hittite monuments

Gausaura

Kumani

· Tyana

ARZAWA?

Sarus R.

Marash

Birejik

MITANNI

Taurus Mts.

Tarsus

Carchemish ·

Til Barsip

Pyramus R.

HARRI

Balikh R.

CILICIA

Halpa (Aleppo)

EUPHRATES R.

SYRIA

Ras Shamra

Orontes R.

Syrian Desert

CYPRUS

MEDITERRANEAN SEA

Kadesh

Byblos

AMORITES

Berytus

PHOENICIA

Sidon

· Damascus

Tyre

· Mt. Hermon

· Kadesh Naphtali

SEA OF GALILEE

Mt. Carmel · Nazareth

Megiddo · Jezreel

SAMARIA

Joppa

· Shiloh

Gath · Bethel

Jerusalem ·

· Jericho

Ascalon

Gaza ·

· Bethlehem

Hebron

DEAD SEA

· Beersheba

PALESTINE

The Phoenicians. The Phoenicians (from the Greek word for "redskins") settled along the coast in what is modern Lebanon. Their principal cities were Sidon, Tyre, Beirut, and Byblos. The Phoenicians helped disseminate Mesopotamian culture through their overseas trading outposts. They established colonies in Spain (Gades, modern Cadiz) and Carthage (modern Tunisia).

The Aramaeans. The Aramaeans were another Semitic people who came out of northern Mesopotamia. They occupied much of Syria, making Damascus their capital. Their language (Aramaic) eventually became the international language of Palestine and Syria. Christ and his disciples spoke Aramaic.

4.2 EARLY ACCOUNTS OF THE HEBREW PEOPLE

The precise origin of the Hebrew tribes is unknown. There are records dating from the Egyptian New Kingdom that mention a homeless nomadic people called the "Habiru" or "Hapiru." Much of the history of the Hebrew people must be pieced together from the Hebrew Scriptures, which were written between the thirteenth and third centuries B.C.E. (ca. 1200-200 B.C.E.). The Hebrew Bible consists of thirty-nine books (nearly two-thirds of the Christian Bible). The Hebrew Scriptures are called the Tanak. The first five books are the Torah (Genesis, Exodus, Leviticus, Numbers, and Deuteronomy). In Greek these books are referred to as the Pentateuch (five books). The Torah tells the story of the origins of the Hebrew people through the forty-year period spent wandering in the desert after their escape from the Pharaoh.

4.3   OUTLINE OF HEBREW HISTORY

4.3.1   *From the Patriarchs to Moses*

According to the Book of Genesis, Abraham left Ur, a city in southern Mesopotamia, sometime between 2000 and 1700 B.C.E. This was roughly contemporaneous with the reign of Hammurabi. Abraham brought his followers to Harram where the Hebrew God was revealed to him. Abraham's grandson, Jacob, led the Hebrew Tribes across the Fertile Crescent to Palestine. Historians speculate that the Hebrew people moved into Egypt during the Hyksos invasion (ca. 1700 B.C.E.). Joseph, Jacob's son, probably served a Hyksos Pharaoh. The resurgence of the Egyptians in the New Kingdom led to the enslavement of the Hebrews (ca. 1500 B.C.E.). During the thirteenth century Moses led the twelve tribes out of Egypt and across the Red Sea into the Sinai wilderness. Around 1200 B.C.E., Joshua led the survivors across the Jordan River into the Land of Canaan (Palestine).

4.3.2   *The Canaanites and the Philistines*

The twelve Hebrew tribes faced two different obstacles in their drive to bring Palestine under their control. Internally, the tribes were divided. They joined together in a loose confederation that was guided by Judges. Externally, the twelve tribes were opposed by two peoples—the Canaanites and the Philistines—who contested the Hebrew claim to Palestine.

Canaan. The Canaanites were a Semitic people who lived in walled cities. Jebus, later renamed Jerusalem by the Hebrews, was one of their urban centers. The Hebrew tribes were unable to dislodge the Canaanites from their fortress cities. Between 1200 and 1000 B.C.E. the Hebrew tribes waged a sporadic war against the Canaanites. During this period the Hebrews possessed no national government.

The Philistines. The arrival of the Philistines sparked the unity that the Hebrew tribes had been unable to create for themselves. Ramses III expelled the Peleset (Philistines) from Egypt sometime after 1100 B.C.E. The Philistines made their capital Gaza. They were technologically superior to their neighbors. By 1050, Philistine soldiers armed with iron weapons had extended their tribe's control over the Hebrew people.

4.3.3 *David*

The loose Hebrew confederation was governed by Judges who served as the arbiters of disputes between the tribes. Late in the eleventh century Saul emerged as King of the unified Hebrew tribes. Saul led the tribes in a revolt against their Philistine overlords. Saul's reign was an unhappy one. His armies failed in their effort to defeat the Philistines, while Samuel (one of the last great Judges) challenged Saul's authority. Saul's death opened the possibility for his son-in-law, David of Bethlehem, to assume command of the Twelve Tribes (1000-961). David vanquished the Philistines. He established the Hebrew capital in Jerusalem. During his reign he had to fight off an unsuccessful revolt against his authority which was led by his son Absolom. He was succeeded by his son Solomon.

4.3.4 *Solomon*

Solomon ruled (961-922 B.C.E.) autocratically but, it is generally agreed, benevolently. He commissioned a tremendous public project of building a Temple and Palace on the summit of Jerusalem. The cost was prohibitive. Each month, 30,000 Hebrew conscripts were sent to Tyre to work in the mines of King Hiram in order to help defray the costs of the buildings. Solomon had 700 wives and 300 concubines. The Tribes broke apart after his death because of the unwillingness of some of their number to accept Solomon's son, Rehoboam, as the next king. Among other factors, Rehoboam may not have been as politically astute as his father; he could not put down a revolt among the tribes of the north, and the kingdom began to break apart.

4.3.5   Israel and Judah

After 922, Palestine was divided into two Hebrew states: Israel and Judah. Ten tribes formed Israel while the remaining two tribes organized themselves into Judah. Israel was wealthier than the more agricultural and pastoral Judah. In 722, the Assyrians conquered Israel. Nothing is known of what became of the Jewish population (Lost Tribes of Israel).

4.3.6   From the Babylonian Captivity to the Diaspora

The poor and less attractive state of Judah continued to exist until 586 when the Chaldeans (New Babylonians) occupied Palestine. King Nebuchadnezzar, the Chaldean King, ordered that several thousand Jews be transported to Babylon (Babylonian Captivity). There they served as advisors and slaves. The Jews preserved their faith and even succeeded in winning Nebuchadnezzar's conversion (Book of Daniel). In 539, the Persians conquered the Chaldeans. Cyrus, the Persian king, allowed the Jews to return to Jerusalem. The Persians tolerated the Jews. Alexander the Great defeated the Persians in Palestine in 325 B.C.E. His successors controlled Jerusalem until 63 B.C.E. when the Romans established a foothold in the Near East. During the Hellenistic period (323-63 B.C.E.) the Jews gained the right to create political corporations (politeuma). The *politeuma* allowed the Jews to govern themselves as a Jewish city within the Hellenistic cities. The Romans restricted Jewish autonomy. In 70 C.E. (Common Epoch), the Jews in Palestine revolted against their Roman governors. The Romans quashed the revolt and ordered the dispersion of the Jews (The Diaspora).

4.4 THE HEBREW RELIGION

Neither the Egyptians nor the Mesopotamians had as substantial an influence on the development of western civilization as the Jews. The unique contribution of the Hebrew civilization was the idea of monotheism. The Hebrew God was neither a natural force nor an anthropomorphic entity. The Jewish conception of God evolved over the course of their history. The Hebrew God placed men and women on earth in order to test their character. This God, Yahweh, was a loving but jealous God who demanded obedience. The essence of the Jewish faith lay in the faithfulness of their covenant-making God, and in His people's obligation to be faithful in turn by upholding His ethical commandments.

4.5 STAGES IN THE DEVELOPMENT OF THE HEBREW CONCEPTION OF GOD

The Hebrew conception of God underwent a complex evolution. At least five distinct phases can be identified.

4.5.1 *Pre-Mosaic* (2000-1250 B.C.E.)

During the earliest period of their development the semi-nomadic Hebrew Tribes practiced animism (worship of spirits dwelling in trees, rocks, and sacred places). Gradually an anthropomorphic conception of a pantheon of gods emerged. God was referred to during this period as "El" (generic word for god). There was no national worship of a single god during this period.

4.5.2 *Henotheism or Period of National Monolatry* (1250-800 B.C.E.)

Moses transformed the Hebrew religion at the beginning of this period. The early Hebrews were henotheists (worshipped their god exclusively but acknowledged that there were other gods). The name of the Hebrew God was Yahweh, which meant literally, "I am what I am."

4.5.3 *The Prophetic Stage* (800-600 B.C.E.)

The Tribes' political disunity and Israel's conquest provoked an outpouring of religious reform. Prophets like Jeremiah, Micah, Hosea, and Isaiah offered explanations for how misfortune had fallen on God's chosen people. The Prophets preached an absolute monotheism. Yahweh was a God of Righteousness who demanded that his followers live according to the Covenant.

4.5.4 *Post-Exilic*

After the return from Babylon, the Hebrew religion continued to evolve. It was a time of continuing challenges to Judaism from within and outside. Widespread assimilation with the peoples of neighboring nations nearly resulted in the loss of the Hebrew language. Around the middle of the fifth century B.C.E., the high priest and scribe Ezra and the political-military leader Nehemiah worked to stanch the decline and bring about the renewal of the kingdom by instituting religious and civic reforms, including the prohibition of intermarriage with non-Jews, and embarking on the rebuilding and refortifying of Jerusalem. Nehemiah reminded the Jews that they owed their redemption as a people—and their freedom from tyranny—to their acceptance of Yahweh's teachings.

4.5.5 *Judaism Under the Romans*

By 30 B.C.E. the Jews were divided into several different sects. The Pharisees (the majority) were drawn from the middle class. They anticipated the coming of a political Messiah who would reestablish the unified Hebrew state that had existed in the time of David and Solomon. The wealthy were followers of the Sadducees. They denied the notion of an afterlife. Finally, the Essenes, an ascetic sect, drew support chiefly from the lower class. The Dead Sea Scrolls (discovered 1948) are believed to contain the Essenes' beliefs.

4.6 THE HEBREW CONTRIBUTION TO CIVILIZATION

4.6.1 *Law*

Many elements of the Deuteronomic Code show the influence of the Code of Hammurabi. The Hebrew conception of law, however, represents a tremendous advance on the lex talionis (law of retribution). God's covenant imposed a tremendous responsibility on his chosen people. Man is conceived as an ethical being who must freely choose to obey or disobey God's laws.

4.6.2 *History*

The Hebrew scriptures present history as a divinely inspired drama. All history represents a struggle to fulfill God's plan. In this struggle man possesses a free will.

4.6.3 *Monotheism*

The single most important contribution of the Jews to western civilization is the concept of monotheism.

CHRONOLOGY OF THE HEBREW CIVILIZATION
(All dates are approximate B.C.E.)

Abraham left Ur	2000 - 1900 B.C.E.
Phoenicians and Aramaeans in Palestine	2000
Jacob into Palestine	1800
Joseph into Egypt	1700
Jews enslaved in Egypt	1500
Moses leads Exodus	1250
Saul first King of Israel	1024 - 1000

Moses leads Exodus	1250		
Saul first King of Israel	1024	-	1000
David's reign	1000	-	961
Solomon and the First Temple	961	-	922
Time of the Prophets	922		
Israel and Judah divide	750	-	430
Israel defeated by Assyrians	722		
Judah falls to the Chaldeans	586		
Babylonian captivity	586	-	539
Persians conquer Chaldeans and allow Jews to return to Jerusalem	538		
Second Temple is built	515		
Alexander conquers Palestine	325		
Ptolemy dynasty controls Palestine	323	-	65
Rome begins conquest of Near East	65		
Jewish Rebellion leads to Diaspora	70	C.E.	

Neo-Babylonian Period: *The Ishtar Gate,* **575 B.C.E. State Museum, East Berlin.**

CHAPTER 5

GREEK CIVILIZATION

5.1 GEOGRAPHY AND CLIMATE

The character of Greek civilization in antiquity was deeply influenced by geography and climate. Running from Mt. Olympus in the north 240 miles southward to the tip of the Peloponnesus, mainland Greece is composed of mountains, plains, valleys, and hills. The scarcity of natural resources compelled the Greeks to fan out across the Aegean. The offshore islands were settled in the Paleolithic Age.

5.2 EARLY AEGEAN CIVILIZATIONS

The Neolithic Revolution occurred later in Greece than it did in the Near East. Archaeologists have uncovered neolithic sites dating to 6500 B.C.E. The early Greeks fashioned tools from obsidian (volcanic rock) because Greece possessed little flint. Between 2600 and 1250 B.C.E. separate civilizations appeared on the mainland and the island of Crete. The seafaring Minoans were centered on Crete while the Mycenaeans developed small fortified cities in the Peloponnesus. Little was known

ANCIENT GREECE

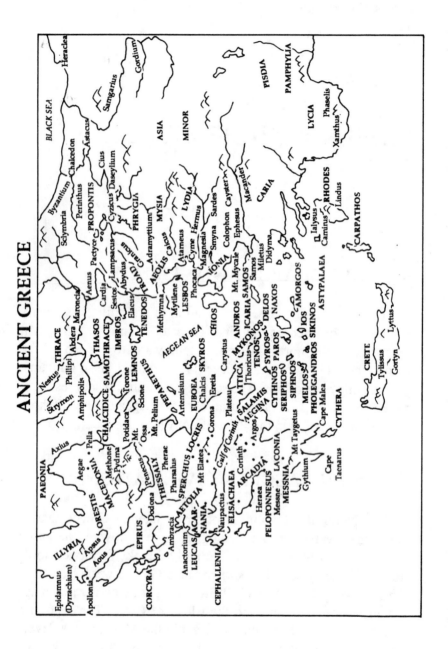

of the Minoans and Mycenaeans until the end of the nineteenth century when the German Heinrich Schliemann, a retired businessman and amateur archaeologist, began excavating in Asia Minor. Schliemann is credited with discovering the site of ancient Troy (the VIIa settlement of nine successive occupations of the same location) and the cyclopean fortress (called cyclopean because of its thick walls) of Mycenaea. Arthur Evans, an English archaeologist, discovered the site of Knossos, the Minoan capital city, in 1900.

5.2.1 *The Minoans* (2600-1250 B.C.E.)

The legendary King Minos (ca. 2000 B.C.E.) supplied Arthur Evans with the name for the seafaring civilization that flourished on the island of Crete. The Minoans entered the Bronze Age around 3000 B.C.E. Crete's geographical position midway between the Greek mainland and Egypt made it an ideal location for the development of a civilization based on overseas trade. The island's population grew during 2900-2100 B.C.E. through the influx of people from Libya and Asia Minor. By 2000 B.C.E. the Minoans had begun construction of a vast palace (eventually more than 250 rooms) in their capital of Knossos. This palace is probably the origin of the idea of the labyrinth that appears in Greek mythology in the story of Theseus and the Minotaur. The high point of the Minoan civilization came between 1600 and 1500 B.C.E. The unfortified character of the Minoan cities suggests that the Minoans were a peaceful people who experienced little domestic unrest and few external adversaries. The Minoans developed several forms of written language. Michael Ventris demonstrated that one of these languages (Linear B) is the ancestor of ancient Greek. Unlike their Near Eastern contemporaries, the Minoan religion was matriarchal. Historians and archaeologists disagree as to the precise fate of the Minoans. Some argue that the Minoan civilization fell victim to mainland invaders. Others contend the civilization was destroyed by a volcanic eruption on the

GREECE IN THE MINOAN AND MYCENAEAN AGE

nearby island of Thera which occurred around 1480 B.C.E. Whatever the precise cause, the Minoan civilization was in a state of decline at the close of the fifteenth century. The great palace at Knossos was destroyed around 1400 B.C.E.

5.2.2 The Mycenaeans

Sometime before 2200 B.C.E. an Indo-European people (Indo-European refers to the linguistic family to which most of the European languages belong) migrated into the Peloponnesus. This people organized their lives around fortresses which were built in high places. The Mycenaeans reached the apex of their development between 1400 and 1230 B.C.E. A king (wanax) who served as the chief military leader and priest led each fortified acropolis (acro is Greek for high; polis means city). Between 1500 and 1200 B.C.E. the Mycenaeans buried their great warriors in circular, beehive-like tombs (tholos). Heinrich Schliemann unearthed the most famous of these tombs (The Treasury of Atreus) during his excavations. The principal Mycenaean cities included Pylos, Argos, and Mycenae.

5.2.3 Influence of the Minoans and Mycenaeans on Greek History

Neither the Minoans nor the Mycenaeans had a direct influence on the subsequent development of western civilization. Nevertheless, the Minoans and the Mycenaeans are important because they were the earliest civilizations to develop in Europe.

5.3 THE GREEK DARK AGES (1200-750 B.C.E.)

Between 1200 and 750 B.C.E., Greece fell into decline. Writing disappeared during this period and was reintroduced around 750 B.C.E.

5.3.1 The Dorians

The Greek Dark Ages were catalyzed in part by the Dorian invasion of mainland Greece and the islands during the twelfth century. The Dorians were a barbaric (uncivilized Greek) people who originated in the mountainous North of Greece. The Dorians occupied all of the Peloponnesus. The Dorian invasion pushed the Ionians (another Greek people) into Attica and across the Aegean to the islands off the coast of Asia Minor. The Dorians were a politically primitive people who followed the Mycenaean pattern and organized themselves into small fortified cities. Dorian cities were loosely organized around a tribal leader (basileus) whose primary responsibilities were military and priestly. Law was determined by custom. The Dorian religion conceived of the world as a place of mystery in which the gods (anthropomorphic entities) exercised a limited influence over human life. The Dorian gods resided on Mt. Olympus and manifested themselves through oracles in sacred places like Delphi, Delos, and Eleusis. Unlike in the Hebrew religion, the Dorians possessed no articles of faith. The Dorians cremated their dead and were generally unconcerned with the afterlife.

5.3.2 Homer and Hesiod

Writing was reinvented during the eighth century. Homer and Hesiod provide us with evidence of the transition from an oral to a literate culture.

Homer. The Homeric poems were really collections of oral epic songs that had existed seperately during the Dark Ages and which told the story of the Greeks' defining experience in the Trojan War. They described warriors who were striving for *arete,* the Greeks' conception of virtue. Virtue was attained through self-knowledge, and signified the excellence that comes from the acquisition of practical wisdom. Religion in Homer's day was also very practical, influencing every aspect of daily life. The gods were expected to provide assistance in day-to-day living, and worship consisted primarily of giving offerings in exchange for guidance for life and healing for the body. In the *Iliad,* Homer narrated a series of episodes in the last year of the Trojan War. The *Odyssey* describes Odysseus's journey from Troy to his home on the island of Ithaca. Homer's epics describe events that occurred at least five centuries before his time. The poems incorporated elements drawn from the post-Mycenaean Age. Homer's heroes are cremated instead of being buried in tholos tombs. In the *Iliad* and *Odyssey*, the gods are worshipped in temples. There were no temples in the Mycenaean world. Homer's warriors do battle in chariots. The chariot was known to the Mycenaeans but was not used in battle. Finally, the power of Homer's kings is restricted when compared to the Mycenaean kings. Thus, Homer's poems present a synthesis of Mycenaean and Dorian elements.

Hesiod. Hesiod was the author of two works that are extant. In his *Works and Days*, he provided a portrait of everyday life. His *Theogony* offers a summary of the principal stories and myths concerning the Olympic gods and their predecessors. The Greeks never possessed a bible. Their religion was based on the stories recounted by Homer and Hesiod.

5.4 THE ARCHAIC PERIOD (800-500 B.C.E.)

Greece was transformed in the period from 800 to 500 B.C.E. Hesiod described the forces that were changing Greece in his *Works and Days*. Population outgrew the available resources. Class struggle emerged. The shortage of land forced the Greek city-states (poleis) to seek alternatives. Three patterns emerged. Some of the city-states established overseas colonies. Corinth followed this route. Others, like Athens, emphasized trade and the development of local industry as an alternative to agriculture. Sparta was unique in that it conquered the neighboring Messenians, thereby gaining a land and people to dominate.

5.4.1 *The Rise of the City-State*

Between 800 and 323 B.C.E., Greek life was organized around the polis or city-state. The polis was a small, closely knit community that provided the basis for every aspect of life.

GREEK COLONIES

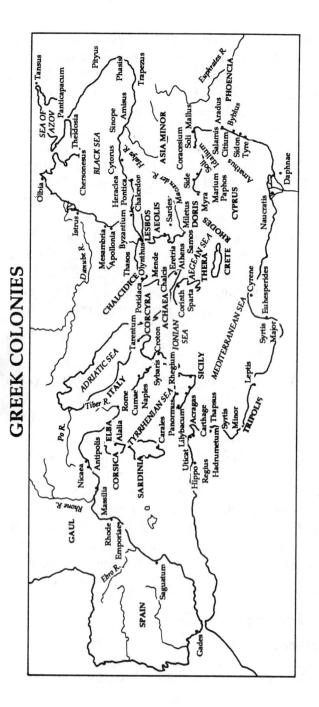

The evolution of the polis followed roughly the same course of development throughout Greece. Apparently, the polis originated as a tribal religious body and was transformed in time into a secular organization. In the eighth century the aristocracy or nobility replaced the monarchies that led most of the poleis. Generally, oligarchs led the city-states until late in the sixth century when they were replaced by tyrants. The word *tyrant* did not carry the pejorative meaning that it has today. To the Greeks, a tyrant was simply an individual who held absolute power. By the end of the sixth century the tyrants were replaced in a number of city-states by democratic governments. Sparta and Athens illustrate the sharp contrasts possible in the development of the polis. Sparta achieved stability at the expense of becoming an armed camp while Athens developed into a community that prided itself in its political freedom.

5.4.2 *Sparta*

Early in the Archaic Period (ca. 800 B.C.E.), Sparta dominated Laconia (the southern Peloponnesus). The Spartans were referred to as the Laconians or Lacedaemonians (the word *laconic,* which means "sparing with words," derives from Laconia). Sparta did not evolve into a democracy. In the seventh century Sparta faced overpopulation and a need for agricultural land. Instead of expanding overseas the Spartans crossed the Taygetus Mountains (ca. 750 B.C.E.) and seized control of Messenia. The plain of Messenia gave the Spartans all the land they would ever need and a population to work it. Sparta included an area of 3,000 square miles. In 650 B.C.E. the Messianians revolted. The revolt was crushed but it left a lasting imprint on Sparta. The Spartans made themselves into an armed camp to prevent future rebellions. The Messenians were collectively owned as serfs of the state (helots). Since the Messenians outnumbered the Spartans ten to one, every Spartan entered a lifetime of military service as a hoplite (warrior) at the age of seven. Twenty-eight elders constituted the governing body from which five elders (ephors) were chosen to administer the state. Spartan society broke into three classes: The Spartans; the *perioeci* ("dwellers around"), or free Greeks, from other poleis who served as artisans and traders; and the helots. Around 640 B.C.E., Lycurgus drew the different elements of the Spartan political and social order together in a constitution. Sparta organized the other Peloponnesian city-states (with the exception of Argos) into the Peloponnesian League in the middle of the sixth century (ca. 550).

5.4.3 *Athens*

Athens was the principal city of Attica (roughly 1,000 square miles). Between 1000 and 700 B.C.E., Athens was governed by monarchs (legendary kings such as Perseus and Theseus). In the eighth century aristocrats replaced the monarchy with an oligarchy. Draco (ca. 621) offered the first codification of Athenian law. The Draconian Code was notorious for its harshness. It favored the propertied and allowed debtors to be sold into slavery. Solon (640-559 B.C.E.) reformed Athens' laws in 594. Solon enfranchised the lower classes and gave the state responsibility for administering justice (Dike). Previously, justice was treated as the will of Zeus and left to individuals and families to enforce. Solon based the idea of justice on the community as a whole. The Athenian governing body was the Council of the Areopagus. Archons (leaders of the polis) were selected from the Areopagus. During the sixth century the position of the nobles was strengthened as the agricultural crisis (insufficient land and growing indebtedness among the small farmers) worsened. Late in the sixth century Peisistratus (605-527 B.C.E.) seized control of the polis, governing as a tyrant. In 527, Cleisthenes led a reform movement that established the basis of Athens' democratic government. To prevent the return of tyranny, Cleisthenes stipulated that the Council of Five Hundred had the power to call an annual assembly to identify individu-

PERSIAN EMPIRE ABOUT 500 B.C.

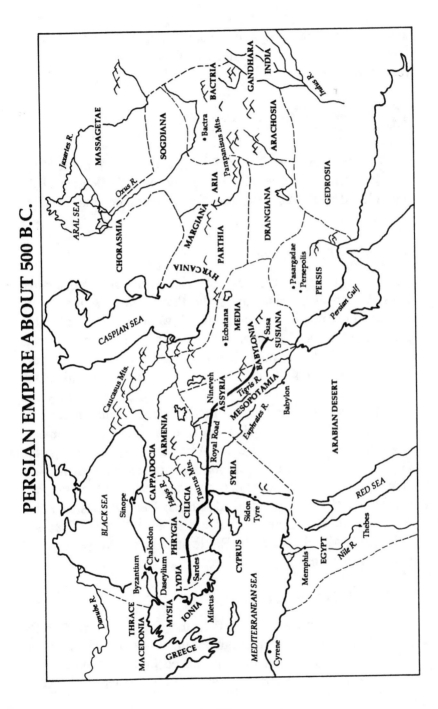

als considered dangerous to the state. The voting was done on "ostraka" (potsherds). The individual who was ostracized was exiled for ten years.

5.5   THE FIFTH CENTURY

The fifth century (Classical Age) was the high point of the Greek civilization. The century opened with the Persian Wars and closed with the disastrous Peloponnesian War between Athens and Sparta.

5.5.1   *The Persian War*

In 499 the Ionian Greeks in Asia Minor rebelled against their Persian overlords. Darius, the Persian king, sent an army to punish the rebels. Athens supplied twenty ships as aid to the Ionians. After the Persian army had crushed the Ionians, Darius decided that Athens must be taught a lesson. In 490 his army met the Athenians at Marathon. At Marathon the Athenians won an important victory. The Persians retreated. Ten years later Darius's son, Xerxes, returned to Greece with an army of 250,000 soldiers. The Persians crossed the Hellespont (the narrow strait separating Europe and Asia) and marched against the Greeks. Three hundred Spartans temporarily blocked the Persian advance at Thermopylae (a mountain pass). When the Persians reached Attica they burned Athens. Themistocles, an Athenian, organized the Greek naval strategy. The Persian fleet was defeated in 479 B.C.E. at the Battle of Salamis. Xerxes ordered his army to retreat.

5.5.2   *The Delian League*

After the victory over the Persians, 150 of the Greek city-states formed the Delian League. Athens was the chief city in the League. The Delian League existed in order to protect its members against the possible return of the Persians. The Athenians manipulated the League to their advantage. Pericles, the leader of Athens, used part of the League's treasury to rebuild Athens (the Parthenon and other major buildings on the Acropolis were constructed during this period). The Spartans feared the Athenians. War was inevitable when the Athenians started construction on a wall around the city and fortifications around their seaport at Piraeus.

5.5.3 The Peloponnesian War (431-404 B.C.E.)

War broke out in 431 B.C.E. Sparta had a bigger army but Athens had a larger fleet. In 430, Spartan hoplites invaded Attica. Athens' situation was made worse by the outbreak of the plague. Thucydides (an Athenian historian) estimated that one third of the population died from the plague (Pericles died of the plague in 429). Neither side possessed sufficient strength to defeat its rival. An armistice was agreed on in 421. The war resumed in 414 because Athens sought to expand its influence in Sicily. Athens lost 50,000 men and 200 ships in their Sicilian Campaign. The war dragged on until 404 when Athens was compelled to accept defeat.

5.5.4 The Decline of Greek City-States

The Peloponnesian War marked the turning point in Greek history. Athens and Sparta had destroyed themselves. Sparta fell victim to Thebes shortly after the war's end. The Greek city-states were unable to see beyond their individual interest. They allowed themselves to be drawn into fratricidal warfare. The inability to work together spelled their doom. In the fourth century the semi-barbarian state of Macedonia marshalled its forces and began its systematic conquest of the Greek city-states, and then, the world.

CHRONOLOGY OF GREECE
(All dates are approximate B.C.E.)

Neolithic age ends	ca. 3000		B.C.E.
Bronze Age civilization	3000	-	1000
Height of Minoan civilization	1600		
Height of Mycenaean civilization	1500	-	1300
Fall of Troy	ca. 1250		
Dorian invasion	ca. 1100		
Greek Dark Ages	1100	-	750
Homer	ca. 780	-	725
First Olympic Games	776		
Hesiod	ca. 750		
Colonization	ca. 750	-	550
Archaic Greek civilization	ca. 750	-	479
Spartan conquest of Messenia	ca. 730		
Draco	621		
Thales, Anaximader, Anaximenes	621	-	500
Croesus of Lydia	550	-	546
Persian conquest of Asiatic Greeks	545		
Aeschylus	ca. 524	-	456
Pindar	ca. 522	-	441
Persian War	499	-	479
Battle of Marathon	490		
Battle of Thermopylae and Salamis	480		
Delian League established	477		
Socrates	469	-	399
Peloponnesian War	431	-	404
Death of Pericles	429		
Plato founds Academy	387		
Philip II of Macedon	359	-	336

CHAPTER 6

THE GREEK CULTURAL ACHIEVEMENT

6.1 FROM MYTH TO REASON

The Greeks were not the first to question the nature of the universe and man's place in it. No other ancient people, however, probed so deeply and allowed their inquiries to range so widely. Between 750 and 323 B.C.E., the Greeks broke from the mythopoetic (myth-making) notions of the Near East and applied human reason to the task of understanding nature and man's place in the cosmos. To the Greeks goes credit for establishing the philosophical framework within which western civilization has developed.

6.1.1 *The Pre-Socratics: The Problem of Cosmology*

The Greeks discovered the problem of cosmology (the Greek word "cosmos" means "order"; "ology" means "study of"). Like the Near Eastern civilizations the Greeks moved from animism to a polytheism in which they conceived of their gods as entities which governed a part of nature (Poseidon for the sea,

Apollo for the sun, etc.) or as having control over a special function (Hermes, the messenger; Aphrodite, love, etc.). During the sixth century several schools of philosophers (the Greek word "philo" means "lover"; "sophe" means "knowledge") appeared in Greece and her colonies. These "lovers of knowledge" made a radical break with their predecessors. They examined the cosmos without making recourse to transcendent or supernatural entities. These philosophers are called the Pre-Socratics because they lived before Socrates' birth (ca. 469 B.C.E.). The earliest of the Pre-Socratics were Ionian Greeks who were concentrated on the Greek islands off the coast of Asia Minor. The first of these philosophers were centered in Miletus (on the west coast of modern Turkey).

6.1.2 The Milesians

Thales of Miletus (ca. 621-548 B.C.E.) was the first philosopher to offer a purely materialistic explanation for natural phenomenon. While most of his contemporaries continued to believe that Poseidon caused earthquakes, Thales proposed a naturalistic explanation. Only a handful of fragments of Thales's works are extant. In one of these fragments Thales declared that "All is Water." Thales was inquiring into the nature of the universe. His answer is purely materialistic and open to examination by his successors. This is what Thales's student, Anaximander (ca. 611-546 B.C.E.), did. He thought that Thales's hypothesis was too narrow. Anaximander proposed that the universe was formed from something he called "the boundless." The central property of the "boundless" was its ability to change. Anaximander is credited with drawing the first map of the world. Another Milesian, Anaximenes (d. 525 B.C.E.), disagreed with both Thales and Anaximander and argued that the primary substance was air. The Milesians revolutionized the study of philosophy because they abandoned the idea that the universe was formed by the arbitrary will of the gods. They sought a rational and materialistic explanation for the nature of things. Perhaps most significant of all, the Milesians' theories were not articles of a religious faith but were subject to testing and modifications by later thinkers.

6.1.3 *The Pythagoreans*

Pythagoras (ca. 580-507 B.C.E.) answered the question of what was the nature of the physical world mathematically. Pythagoras gathered a group of his followers in the Greek colony of Croton in southern Italy. Pythagoras believed that numbers and geometrical forms were primary. Matter originated in number. This led the Pythagoreans to seek the mathematical ratios and perfect numbers that underpinned existence. Pythagoras is usually credited with introducing the study of metaphysics ("meta" is Greek for "beyond"; "physics" means "things").

6.1.4 *Parmenides and Heraclitus*

Parmenides and Heraclitus represent two different tendencies in the Pre-Socratics. Parmenides (ca. 515-450 B.C.E.) opposed both the materialism of the Milesians and the formism or idealism of the Pythagoreans. Parmenides was the founder of the study of formal logic. He believed that stability or permanence was the true nature of things. To Parmenides the business of philosophy was to penetrate through the appearance of change. Heraclitus (ca. 500 B.C.E.) held that every single thing was in a process of continuous change. Heraclitus warned that sense data must not be accepted blindly.

6.1.5 *Empedocles, Leucippus, and Democritus*

Empedocles (ca. 495-430 B.C.E.), Leucippus (ca. 450 B.C.E.), and Democritus (ca. 460-370 B.C.E.) can be grouped with the Pre-Socratics even though they were Socrates's contemporaries because of their interest in cosmological questions. Empedocles sought to reconcile the position of those who believed that "Being," or essence, was the nature of the universe (Milesians) with Heraclitus's notion that "Becoming" or change was the basis of all things. Empedocles argued that there were four primary elements: earth, water, air, and fire. Empedocles believed that the twin forces of Love and Hate were constantly working to combine and separate the primary elements. Leucippus argued that nature was divided into empty space and an infinite number of atoms ("atomon" in Greek means indivisible). Leucippus believed that gravity caused the atoms to form different arrangements. This accounts for the differences between physical objects. Democritus was Leucippus's student. He is credited with taking his teacher's ideas and building them into a system.

6.2 THE AGE OF SOCRATES: FROM COSMOLOGY TO ETHICS

6.2.1 *The Sophists*

The defeat of the Persians and the ascendancy of Athens among the Greek poleis produced a revolution in Greek philosophy. The Sophists ("those who were wise") turned away from the physical world and cosmological questions and emphasized the individual. They travelled between the different city-states teaching rhetoric, grammar, music, and mathematics. Their goal was to cultivate the individual's *arete,* or excellence as a citizen of the polis. Protagoras (mid-fifth century), spoke for many of the Sophists when he declared, "Man is the measure of all things."

6.2.2 *Socrates* (ca. 469-399 B.C.E.)

Socrates attacked the Sophists. Nothing of Socrates' teachings has survived except what his students Plato and Xenophon recorded. Apparently, Socrates criticized the Sophists for undermining truth through their emphasis on rhetoric and persuasion. Socrates did not present a systematic theory. Instead he engaged in a continuous process of questioning (dialectics) which took the form of dialogues with his followers. In 399 B.C.E., Socrates was accused of corrupting Athens' youth. He was tried, convicted, and made to drink hemlock (a lethal poison). His conviction was caused by his friendship with the aristocratic party that had seized control of Athens after the city's defeat in the Peloponnesian War.

6.2.3 *Plato* (ca. 429-347 B.C.E.)

Plato developed Socrates' philosophy into a system. Like Socrates, Plato emphasized the study of ethics. He founded the Academy in Athens as a school for the study of philosophy. The main themes in Plato's philosophy revolve around his Theory of Ideas or Forms. Plato believed that there was a higher order behind the apparent flux of external events. What we see is but a dim shadow of the eternal Forms or Ideas. The goal of philosophy was to penetrate through the realm of everyday appearances to the real nature of things. It follows from this that Plato criticized the Sophists for cultivating the study of appearances in their interest of rhetoric. In the *Republic*, Plato developed his conception of the ideal state. Plato built his state on a theory of education. He believed that each individual possessed three capacities: Reason, Spirit, and Appetite. In some individuals one capacity predominates. Accordingly, Plato divided the polis into three classes: the philosophers (reason), the warriors (spirit), and the middle class (appetite). Each class should receive an education that is suited to its nature. The objective of Plato's *Republic* is a state which is ruled by philosopher kings.

6.2.4 *Aristotle* (ca. 384-322 B.C.E.)

Aristotle attended Plato's Academy for twenty years. He criticized his teacher's theory of knowledge, arguing that Forms or Ideas did not exist outside of things. Aristotle contended that it was necessary to consider four factors in treating any object: 1) its matter; 2) its form; 3) what caused it to come into being; and 4) its end or purpose. Aristotle built his philosophical system on an examination of these four causes. He divided philosophy into three parts: Theoretical, Practical, and Productive. Theoretical philosophy included mathematics, logic, metaphysics, and the philosophy of nature (physics, biology, etc.). Practical philosophy consisted of ethics and politics. Productive philosophy referred to poetics and rhetorics. Aristotle left the Academy after Plato's death. He travelled in Asia Minor and the Greek islands collecting data for his empirical studies. Philip of Macedon invited Aristotle to tutor his son Alexander. When Alexander ascended to the throne, Aristotle returned to Athens and opened a school, the Lyceum, outside the city's gates.

6.3   GREEK ART

6.3.1   *The Plastic Arts: Sculpture, Architecture, and Painting*

Greek art during the Minoan and Mycenaean period was influenced by the Mesopotamians and the Egyptians. During the Archaic Period (800-500 B.C.E.) this influence waned as the Greeks developed indigenous art forms. Statues continued to show the rigid formality of Egyptian sculpture well into the seventh century. In vase painting and architecture the Archaic Greeks broke from the Near Eastern patterns. Vases in the seventh century present black figures against a red background. From about 530 B.C.E. this is reversed, with red figures depicted on a black background. Two distinctive architectural orders appeared during this period: The Doric and the Ionic.

Greek art during the classical age (479-401 B.C.E.) emphasized man's individuality and central position in the universe.

THE DORIC AND IONIC ORDERS

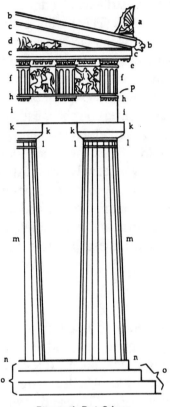

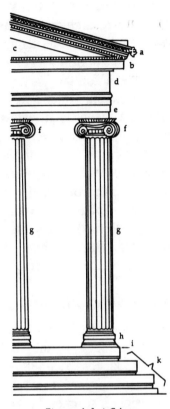

Diagram of a Doric Column
and Entablature

Diagram of a Ionic Column
and Entablature

a Corner Akroterion
b Sima with a lion's head as waterspout
c Geison (cornice)
d Tympanum
e Mutule with Guttae (drops)
f Triglyphs
g Metopes
h Regulae with guttae
i Architrave or Epistyle
k Abacus
l Echinum
m Shaft with 20 sharp-edged flutinys
n Stylobate
o Krepis or Krepidoma
p Tania

a Sima
b Geison
c Tympanum
d Frieze
e Architrave or Epistyle
   (in three parts)
f Capital with Volutes
g Shaft with 24 flutings
   separated by fillets
h Attic Base with double
   Torus and a Trochilos
j Stylobate
k Krepis or Krepidoma

Corinthian Capital

Pericles (leader of Athens until 429 B.C.E.) ordered that Athens' acropolis be rebuilt. Construction on the Parthenon (Ictinus and Callicrates, architects) was begun in 447. The building was dedicated nine years later. The greatest of the Greek sculptors during this period was Phidias. Phidias created a colossal statue of Athena for the Parthenon's main room. This statue is no longer extant. Other new buildings followed. Pericles commissioned a magnificent gateway (the Propylaea) on the west side of the acropolis. Even the expenses of the Peloponnesian War did not call a halt to the work. In 423 B.C.E. the small Ionic temple to Athena Nike was dedicated. Two years later the Athenians began construction on the Erectheum to commemorate the Peace of Nicias. Work on the Erectheum (to the goddess Athena Polias) broke off and the temple was not completed until 409 B.C.E. Much of the funds for these projects were embezzled from the Delian League.

6.3.2   Greek Literature: Poetry

Homer established the basis for the epic tradition in the eighth century. In the sixth century Sappho (ca. 600 B.C.E.) and Pindar (ca. 518-438 B.C.E.) wrote lyrical poems (the word "lyrical" originated in the Greek word "lyre" which referred to a musical instrument). Sappho's poems treated love and friendship while Pindar praised athletic prowess.

6.3.3   Tragedy

The origins of Greek drama are obscure. The earliest dramas were part of religious festivals for the vegetative god Dionysus. The word tragedy is thought to have originated in a Greek word which means "goat song." These "goat songs" were sung by a chorus. During the Archaic Period these religious rituals evolved into festivals where dramas were presented. Thespis introduced a single actor in the sixth century. Classical tragedy appeared in the fifth century. Tragedies were presented at festivals that were held either once or twice a year. Each playwright presented three tragedies and one satyr play (comedy). The audience consisted of the male citizens of the polis. Judges selected one individual to receive a laurel wreath for having presented the best tragedies. Less than twenty tragedies have survived from the classical period.

Aeschylus (525-456 B.C.E.). Aeschylus was the earliest and most conservative of the Greek tragedians. His plays focus on the problem of *hubris* (overweening pride and arrogance). The most famous of Aeschylus's works is the *Orestria* trilogy: *Agamemnon, The Libation Bearers*, and *The Eumenides*.

Sophocles (496-406 B.C.E.). Sophocles is credited with introducing a second actor to Greek tragedy. In his most famous play *Oedipus Rex*, he uses irony to explore the fate of Oedipus.

Euripides (485-406 B.C.E.). Some critics consider Euripides the most modern of the tragedians because he seems the most psychologically minded. Euripides wrote during the Peloponnesian War. In his surviving works there is a sense that man is sometimes the victim of dark forces that are out of his control.

6.3.4 *Comedy*

Aristophanes (ca. 448-390 B.C.E.) pioneered the development of comedy. He used his comedies to oppose Socrates and those who he believed were undermining the polis. During the fourth century, Menander (ca. 342-291 B.C.E.) abandoned political themes that were central to Old Comedy. The New Comedy focused on domestic and individual situations in which typically lovers are blocked by interfering parents.

6.4   HISTORY

The Greeks were the first to develop the study of history. The Mesopotamians, Egyptians, and Jews recorded the exploits of their gods and semi-divine rulers. Herodotus (ca. 484-424 B.C.E.) is usually described as the "father of history." In his *History of the Persian Wars*, he examined human actions. His history is unique in that he treats both the Greeks and Persians sympathetically. Herodotus travelled throughout the ancient world asking questions. He applied the test of his reason to what he was told and discounted what he believed fanciful. Thucydides (ca. 460-400 B.C.E.) developed Herodotus's skeptical nature into the historian's critical attitude. His *History of the Peloponnesian War* described the war's origin and development. Thucydides criticized both his native Athens and Sparta. His goal was to present a rational and empirical history. There was no place in his work for myth.

6.5   THE GREEK ACHIEVEMENT

The Greeks created the framework in which much of western civilization was to develop. In philosophy they turned away from myth and religion to examine the physical nature of the universe. They were the first logicians and metaphysicians. They pioneered the study of rhetoric, politics, and ethics. In their art they presented a vision which emphasized the individual. Their greatness was tied to their conception of the polis as a civilizing force. Their decline was caused by their inability to rise above the rivalries which separated the city-states and create a panhellenic state.

CHAPTER 7

THE HELLENISTIC AGE

7.1   DEFINITION OF HELLENISM

"Hellenism" is a term that was first used in the nineteenth century to describe the three centuries separating Alexander the Great (d. 323 B.C.E.) and the formation of the Roman Empire (27 B.C.E.). During this period Greek culture spread from its Mediterranean base eastwards to the Indus River Valley and westwards to the Atlantic. Hellenism represented the fusion of the Greek and Near Eastern civilizations.

7.2   THE ORIGINS OF HELLENISM (401-336 B.C.E.)

7.2.1   *The Rise of Macedonia*

The decline of the Greek city-states in the fourth century signalled the beginning of a new phase in world history. While Athens and Sparta were destroying one another in the Peloponnesian War, the northern Greek Kingdom of Macedonia was consolidating its power. Macedonia was on the periphery of

THE HELLENISTIC WORLD

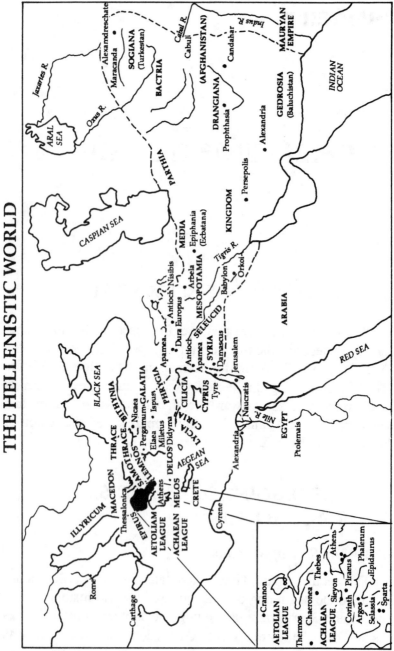

Greece. The Macedonians were a Greek people who were considered semi-barbaric by their southern relatives. Their polis or city-state system never developed in Macedonia. Thus, Macedonia possessed a larger population and more territory than any of the poleis.

7.2.2 *Philip II* (Reign 359-336 B.C.E.)

The quarrels between the Greek city-states made them vulnerable to Macedonian expansionism. In 359 B.C.E., Philip II became King of Macedonia. He needed a seaport on the Aegean and money to finance his state. Three years as a hostage in Thebes (367-364 B.C.E.) had made him sensitive to the weaknesses of the Greek poleis. Between 357 and 336, Philip launched a series of successful campaigns against individual city-states. The city-states were unable to see beyond their own interests and join together to block Philip's advance. Athens' response to Philip's expansionist program was typical. Demosthenes (ca. 384-322 B.C.E.), the orator, tried to alert his countrymen while the leader of another rhetorical school, Isocrates (ca. 436-338 B.C.E.), applauded Philip's actions. Athens was conquered in 338 B.C.E. Philip maintained the fiction that the city-states were independent. He claimed for himself the title of "hegemon" (warlord). Philip was assassinated in 336 B.C.E., two years after launching a war against Persia.

7.3 ALEXANDER THE GREAT (ca. 356-323 B.C.E.)

7.3.1 *Youth and Ascension to the Throne*

Little is known about Alexander's childhood except for his close attachment to his mother and that Aristotle served as his tutor between 343 and 341 B.C.E. Alexander ascended to the throne under suspicious circumstances. Philip had cast off

ALEXANDER'S MILITARY CAMPAIGNS

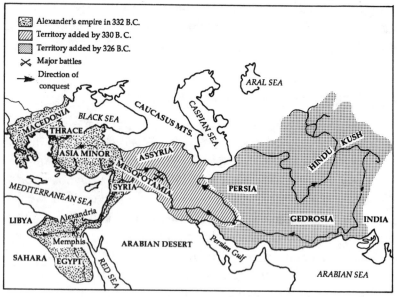

Alexander's mother and married another woman shortly before his death. Whatever his role in his father's death, Alexander surely killed or exiled rival claimants to the throne.

7.3.2 Alexander's Campaigns

Once Alexander had put his own house in order, he resumed his father's war against Persia. In 334 B.C.E., Alexander led 34,000 troops across the Hellespont into Asia Minor. By 333 he had conquered Syria. Three years later he defeated the Persians (at Gaugameia) and occupied the Persian capital of Persepolis. Alexander continued his drive to the east, passing through the Kyber Pass into the Indus River Valley. In 325 B.C.E. his troops threatened to mutiny; they demanded that Alexander allow them to return to Macedonia. Alexander brought his army back to Babylon in 324. Apparently, he decided to organize a new army in hopes of freeing himself from dependence on Macedonian troops whose ties to him could now said to be open to doubt.

Given those circumstances, he took other measures to further consolidate his power and authority. Among them: marrying a Persian princess and ordering eighty of his generals to do likewise. Alexander died of a fever in 323 B.C.E. before he was able to put most of his new plans into action.

7.3.3 Alexander's Legacy

Alexander died without a plan for succession. One tradition has it that on his deathbed he bequeathed his realm "to the strongest." His death provoked an immediate struggle between his most powerful generals. Alexander was one of the greatest military commanders in history. Later commentators have argued that his marrying a Persian princess and encouraging his officers and troops to intermarry with the local populations give evidence that Alexander held a vision of the unity of mankind. Nonetheless, it is more likely that these steps were part of Alexander's plan to strengthen his army. At the time of his death Alexander had established seventy cities and created a trading network that reached from the Mediterranean across the Near East to India.

7.4 OUTLINE OF HELLENISTIC POLITICAL AND SOCIAL HISTORY

7.4.1 The Successor States

Alexander's realm was divided among three of his high-ranking generals. Seleucus established a dynasty in Persia, Mesopotamia, and Syria; Ptolemy seized control of Phoenicia, Palestine, and Egypt; and Lysimachus governed Asia Minor and Macedonia. In Greece a number of the poleis rebelled against the Macedonians. They formed the Achaean and Aetolian Leagues. These confederations were the closest the Greeks ever came to achieving national unity until modern times. By 30 B.C.E. each of the successor states had fallen to Rome.

7.4.2 Government and Society

The polis was the basis of society in a classical world. In the Hellenistic Age the role of the city-state was eclipsed. Alexander's conquests created a trading network that generated an economic transformation throughout Greece and the Near East. Wealth and the ownership of land was increasingly concentrated in the aristocracy. This gulf between the rich and poor grew wider. The influx of Persian gold into Europe at the end of the fourth century caused an inflationary cycle in which wages lagged behind the rising cost of living. Economic historians have demonstrated that wages in Athens during the third century were only fifty percent of what they were during the Age of Pericles, while the cost of living was considerably higher.

7.5 HELLENISTIC CULTURE

7.5.1 Literature

The creation of a vast Library and Museum (from the Greek "Muses," who were nine goddesses for literature, the arts, and sciences) in Alexandria early in the third century had tremendous consequences. The Museum was a place in which scientists and inventors conducted experiments. The Library eventually held more than 300,000 papyrus scrolls. Callimachus (ca. 305-240) was one of the first librarians. He opened what was to be the first chapter in the debate between the ancients and the moderns. Callimachus believed that it was impossible to write epic works equal to the archaic Greeks. His contemporary Apollonius (ca. 295 B.C.E.) accepted his challenge and wrote the *Argonautica,* which told the story of Jason's quest for the Golden Fleece. Meander (ca. 342-291 B.C.E.) shifted the focus of comedy away from political satire to the portrayal of human frailty in marriage and everyday life. Polybius (ca. 200-118 B.C.E.) was the most important historian during the Hellenistic period. Taken captive by the Romans during the Second Macedonian

War, Polybius shifted the focus of history from the story of a single polis to examine the rise of Rome to a position as a world-state. Polybius was a critical historian who built his narrative on eyewitness accounts and who carefully checked his sources.

7.5.2 Philosophy: The Major Trends

The Hellenistic Age produced two major and two minor additions to the history of philosophy. Epicureanism and Stoicism represented the period's dominant philosophical movements. Skepticism and Cynicism found limited support among those unwilling to accept the Epicureans, and Stoics, confidence in reason. Hellenistic philosophy marked a turning point in the western intellectual tradition. The classical Greek philosophers linked the individual's happiness to the community's well-being. The philosophers of the Hellenistic period focused on the individual. The business of philosophy shifted from the pursuit of knowledge for its own sake. The goal of philosophy became the individual's peace of mind and personal happiness.

Epicureanism. Epicurus (ca. 342-270 B.C.E.) founded a school in Athens and based his metaphysics on Democritus's atomic theory. Epicurus taught that the goal of philosophy should be to help the individual find happiness. Unlike Socrates and Plato, he did not make citizenship in a polis the basis of happiness. Epicurus argued that a wise man eschewed public affairs and sought self-sufficiency. Later critics accused Epicurus and his followers of advocating a life based on pursuing the pleasures of the flesh. To Epicurus, however, the highest pleasure was to be found in contemplation.

Stoicism. Zeno (ca. 335-263 B.C.E.) established a rival philosophical school under the *Stoa Poikile* (painted porch) of the Athenian *Agora* (marketplace). There are a number of similarities between Stoicism and Epicureanism. Like Epicurus, Zeno

73

emphasized the importance of the individual. Moreover, both schools were based on a materialistic metaphysics and claimed universal validity for their teachings. There were, however, significant differences between the two philosophical outlooks. Zeno taught that the cosmos was a unified whole which was based on a universal order (Logos or Fire). Every man carried a spark of this Logos in his reason. At death this spark returned to its origin. The Stoics taught that each person should strive to discover the natural law governing the universe and live in accordance with it.

Skepticism and Cynicism. The Skeptics attacked the Epicureans and the Stoics. Carneades of Cyrene (ca. 213-129 B.C.E.) argued that all knowledge was relative. The sensory impressions which we receive from the external world are flawed. Individuals should abandon the quest for knowledge because nothing can be known for certain. The safest course is to doubt everything. Indifference is the only philosophically defensible position. Diogenes of Sinope (d. 323 B.C.E.) was the most famous cynic. His goal was to prepare the individual for any disaster. He lived as a beggar and was famous for his outspoken condemnation of sham and hypocrisy. One story has it that when he met Alexander the Great and the world-conqueror asked him what he wanted, Diogenes replied that Alexander should get out of his light.

7.5.3 *Hellenistic Science*

The scientific and technological accomplishments of the Hellenistic Age were not equalled until the scientific revolution of the seventeenth century. Several factors account for this burst of scientific activities. Alexander the Great supported scientific research. Engineers, astronomers, scientists, and historians accompanied his armies on their campaigns. Moreover, Alexander's victories won Hellenistic natural philosophers access to Egyptian and Chaldean records. Technological developments were encouraged by the growing appetite for material comfort and practical knowledge. Important advances occurred in all the sciences.

Mathematics and Astronomy. Euclid's (ca. 310-230 B.C.E.) *Elements of Geometry* provided the essentials of plane and solid geometry. Apollonius of Perga (flourished 240-200 B.C.E.) was known as the "great geometer" because of his work on conic sections. The advances in geometry kindled a new interest in astronomy. Heraclides of Pontus (ca. 390-310 B.C.E.) proposed that Mercury and Venus orbit the sun. Aristarchus of Samos (ca. 310-230 B.C.E.) presented a heliocentric (sun-centered) theory of the solar system. Hipparchus (b. 190) reverted to a geocentric (earth-centered) solar system while successfully applying trigonometry to the problem of calculating the equinoxes and the length of the year. Ptolemy (second century of the Common Epoch) was the greatest of the Hellenistic astronomers. He systematized Hellenistic astronomy in his *Almagest* (Arabic, meaning "The Greatest Book"). The *Almagest* served as the basis of astronomy until the sixteenth century.

Geography and Medicine. Eratosthenes (ca. 276-190 B.C.E.) pioneered the study of geography. Eratosthenes succeeded in calculating the circumference of the Earth (within two hundred miles) and devised the system of longitude and latitude. Herophilus (fl. 300 B.C.E.) was the first anatomist to perform public dissections. His contemporary, Erasistratus of Chios (fl. 300-260 B.C.E.), opened the study of physiology by tracing the path of veins and arteries through the body. Herophilus and Erasistratus were members of the Dogmatic School of Medicine in which speculation guided research. Galen (129-199 C.E.) was the most important of the Hellenistic medical practitioners. His theories influenced medical practice from antiquity to modern times. Galen followed Aristotle's division of earthly creatures into three types: vegetative, sensitive, and rational. Man was unique in that he possessed all three faculties. Galen's innovation was that he argued that each of these faculties was represented respectively in the digestive, respiratory, and nervous systems.

Physics. Archimedes (ca. 287-212 B.C.E.) is credited with the discovery of the science of hydrostatics, the principle of the lever, the pulley, and the screw. Archimedes invented the astronomer's cross-staff and devised a method of calculating *pi* (the ratio of the circumference of a circle to its diameter) which could be calculated to whatever degree of accuracy that was desired. Hero of Alexandria (first century B.C.E.) applied his talent to military engineering, making scientific instruments, and creating ingenious toys. Notable among his hundreds of inventions are: the fire engine, the siphon, a water clock, a Dioptra (early surveying instrument), and a catapult that was operated by forced air.

7.5.4 *Hellenistic Religion*

Religious practices varied greatly during the Hellenistic Age. The upper classes were attracted to Stoicism and Epicureanism. The expansion of trade produced an exchange of ideas which brought Near Eastern religious practices into the Mediterranean world. The Egyptian cult of Isis (Egyptian fertility goddess), Serapis (invented by King Ptolemy as a hybrid of Osiris and Zeus worship) and Mithraism (a variant of Zorastrianism) won many followers. It was during this period that the Hebrew Scriptures were translated into Greek.

7.6 THE LEGACY OF THE HELLENISTIC AGE

In some respects the Hellenistic Age resembles the modern world. This period showed a tremendous variety of philosophical systems and religious beliefs. It witnessed the expansion of trade and the eclipse of the city-state. Wealth and individual happiness were viewed as life's chief objective. Simultaneously, the Hellenistic Age showed tremendous interest in science and technology.

Demeter, from the temple of the Greek goddess of agriculture at Cnidus, ca. 340-330 B.C.E. Marble. British Museum, London.

CHAPTER 8

THE ROMAN REPUBLIC

8.1 GEOGRAPHY

Italy occupies an area of approximately 90,000 square miles running 720 miles from the Alps in the north to the tip of the peninsula. Italy is 320 miles wide between the Alps and the Apennines Mountains (where the peninsula begins). From the Apennines southward the peninsula is never more than 125 miles wide. Except for several remarkable deposits of marble, Italy possesses few natural resources. The mild Mediterranean climate and the quality of the land made Italy ideal for the development of agriculture in prehistoric times.

8.1.1 *The Early Italians*

The Neolithic Revolution occurred around 2500 B.C.E. in Italy. Italy entered the Bronze Age around 1500 B.C.E. By 1000 B.C.E., the early Italians were making tools and weapons out of iron. The first Italians occupied the highland pastures. These peoples included the Umbrians, Sabines, Sammites, Latins, and others. All of these peoples spoke variants of the Italic language, the ancestor of modern Italian.

ITALY IN THE SIXTH CENTURY

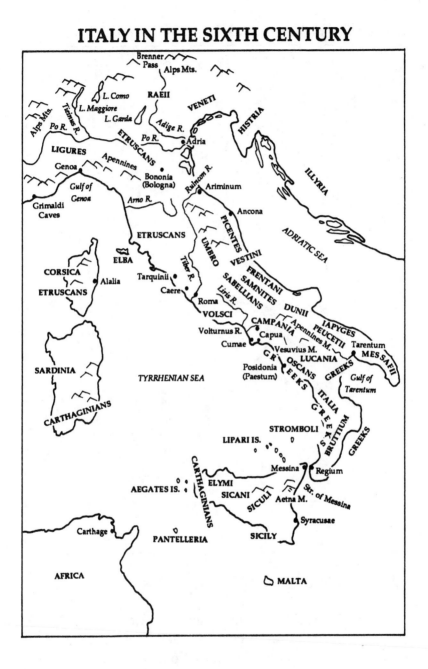

THE FOUNDING OF ROME

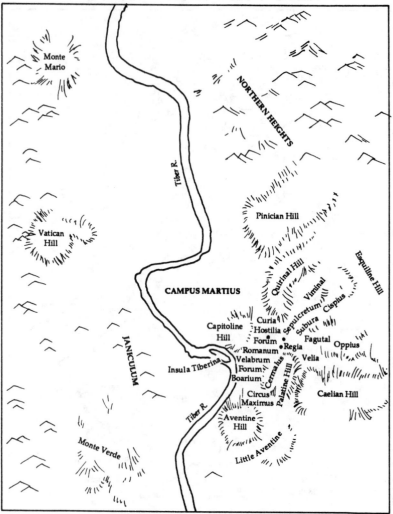

8.2   THE FOUNDING OF ROME

The traditional date for the founding of Rome is 753 B.C.E. Rome is located on seven hills 15 miles from the point where the Tiber River flows into the sea. Rome's location made it a natural center for trade and communications.

8.2.1 *The Etruscans and the Greeks*

Early Rome was influenced by the Greeks and the Etruscans. Between 800 and 500 B.C.E. the Greeks established colonies in southern Italy and Sicily. The Romans adopted their alphabet from the Greeks and incorporated much of the Greek conception of the gods into their religious practices. The Etruscans exercised an even more important influence on the Romans. The origin of the Etruscans is unknown. Around 800 B.C.E. they settled between the Arno and Tiber Rivers in what is now Tuscany. In the seventh and sixth centuries the Etruscans expanded southward, conquering Rome and the other Italic tribes.

8.3 THE ROMAN REPUBLIC

8.3.1 *The Creation of the Republic*

Late in the sixth century (the traditional date is 509 B.C.E.) the Romans expelled the Etruscans. The monarchy was overthrown and an aristocratically based Republic was established. (The Roman rebellion was supposedly provoked by the rape of a virtuous Roman matron, Lucretia, by an Etruscan from the Tarquin family.)

8.3.2 *Government*

In the early Republic, power was concentrated in the patricians (land-owning aristocrats). The Republic was governed by a Senate which was comprised of one hundred (later 300) patricians. The Senate selected two of its members to serve as Consuls for a one year term. The Republic placed vast power in its executives (the imperium). Two quaestors (financial officials) helped the consuls manage the Republic's economic affairs. Theoretically, the consuls' actions had to be approved by the Senate and ultimately by the Assembly, which represented all the people. In practice the early consuls possessed near-despotic power. In times of crisis one of the consuls received six months of authority to govern as a dictator.

8.3.3 *Roman Society*

Roman society was based on the family. The father's prerogatives were similar to the state's imperium. A father could sell his children into slavery. Wives had limited rights. Outside the family a system of clientage knitted the society together. The client was an inferior who was under the protection of someone more powerful. A client was said to be in his patron's "fides" (trust). The client/patron relationship passed through generations.

8.3.4 *The Struggle of the Orders*

Contention between the patricians and plebians (some wealthy families and the majority of the common people) marked the history of the early Republic. The plebians deeply resented the patricians' advantages. Between 509 and 287 B.C.E. the plebians succeeded in winning a share of the power. The plebians won their first victory in 494 B.C.E. when the Senate granted the tribes (areas of the city) the right to elect Tribunes to represent the plebians in disputes with patricians' magistrates. A second victory came in 450 B.C.E. with the publication of the Law of the Twelve Tablets (called this because the laws were written on wooden tablets). The Twelve Tablets codified the people's traditional rights. In 367 B.C.E. the Senate broke with tradition and elected a plebian Consul. In 287 B.C.E. the plebians won their most important victory. Henceforth, the plebian Assembly's acts were to be considered binding and not subject to the Senate's veto.

8.4 ROME'S EXPANSION UNDER THE REPUBLIC (509-44 B.C.E.)

In their first three centuries the Romans divided their efforts between farming and conquering their neighbors. Rome grew from an insignificant city-state into a world state in three distinctive stages: first, the Romans subjugated the other Italic peoples and brought Italy under their control; second, they defeated Carthage in the Punic wars; and finally, the Romans conquered the Hellenistic successor states in the east while sending Roman armies into the barbarian west.

8.4.1 The Conquest of Italy (509-264 B.C.E.)

Rome conquered Italy through a mixture of diplomatic skill and force. Shortly after the expulsion of the Etruscans, the Romans began to draw their Latin neighbors into coalitions. When entreaties failed, the Romans used their army. Rome's policy toward the other Italic peoples varied. Some were granted full citizenship. Those further from Rome were given municipal status. By 264 Rome had defeated the last of its adversaries on the Italian peninsula and had resolved the internal domestic struggle between the patricians and the plebians.

8.4.2 The Punic Wars (264-146 B.C.E.)

Rome fought three wars against Carthage. The Phoenicians founded Carthage around 800 B.C.E. as a trading outpost. Carthage grew in importance. In 264 there were five major powers in the ancient world: the Seleucid Dynasty in the Near East; the Ptolemies in Egypt and Palestine; the Kingdom of Macedonia; Carthage; and Rome. Two of the powers, Rome and Carthage, were locked in a struggle for control of the Mediterranean. The leaders of the Senate who favored war believed that victory over Carthage would open the path to Rome's hegemony in the ancient world.

The First Punic War (264-241 B.C.E.). The First Punic War ("Punic" because the Romans called Carthage "Phoeni") began when Carthage tried to dominate the eastern Sicilian cities of Messana and Syracuse. Rome allied itself with the Sicilians and war broke out. Rome had a superior land force while Carthage possessed a greater fleet. To win the War, Rome was forced to fight at sea as well as on land. In 257 B.C.E., Rome won an important naval victory and landed an army near Carthage. The Carthagenians repulsed the Romans. The First Punic War continued for sixteen years. Rome's objectives grew as the war progressed. In 241 B.C.E. Carthage agreed to Rome's terms. In the peace treaty Carthage relinquished its interest in Sicily and the other islands between Italy and Sicily. Additionally, Carthage agreed to pay war reparations.

The Second Punic War (218-201 B.C.E.). The peace treaty at the end of the First Punic War was not unduly harsh. The Second Punic War would never have occurred if both parties had conscientiously tried to abide by its terms. This was not to be the case. Initially, the Romans were preoccupied in continuing their campaign against the Gauls in northern Italy. In 238, Rome used a rebellion of Carthage's mercenaries in Sardinia as a pretext to seize the island and demand an additional war payment from Carthage. During this period Carthage sought to recoup its losses by expanding its influence in Spain. In 218 B.C.E., the Romans sent an ultimatum to Hannibal, who was the leader of the Punic forces in Spain. They demanded that Hannibal acknowledge Rome's interest in Spain. Hannibal refused and the Second Punic War began. In the Second Punic War, Rome controlled the seas. This forced Hannibal to attack Rome overland. Hannibal led an army of 26,000 troops and 60 elephants across the Alps and into Italy. Once in Italy he rallied 15,000 more soldiers to his side and marched on Rome. The Republic barely escaped defeat during the next ten years. Hannibal's greatest victory over Rome was at Cannae. In 212

B.C.E., Publicus Scipio (ca. 237-183 B.C.E.) was given proconsular status in Spain. Two years later he defeated the main Punic army. By 202 B.C.E. he had carried the war to Africa. The victory of Scipio's army in the Battle of Zama (202 B.C.E.) made Carthage's surrender in 201 B.C.E. inevitable. The Second Punic War had tremendous consequences for Rome. It gave Rome control of Spain and the western Mediterranean. The Peace Treaty eliminated Carthage as Rome's rival. Carthage was reduced to the status of a minor state.

The Third Punic War (149-146 B.C.E.). The Second Punic War left Rome in control of the western Mediterranean. During the War Philip V of Macedonia allied himself with Carthage. This provoked three wars between the Macedonians and the Romans. (First Macedonian War, 215-205 B.C.E.; Second Macedonian War, 200-196 B.C.E.; and Third Macedonian War, 171-167 B.C.E.) These wars had the net effect of extending Rome's influence to the east while bringing Hellenistic culture to Rome. Shiploads of Greek artifacts and slaves who served as teachers and the interpreters of Greek culture were brought to Rome during this period. Rome's final campaign against Carthage came in 149 B.C.E. Despite the fact that Carthage had lived up to the peace treaty, the Roman's hatred of Carthage remained unshaken. Cato the Elder (a Roman Senator) exemplified this. Cato ended every speech he delivered in the Senate – no matter what the topic – with the sentence "Carthage must be destroyed." In 146 the Romans burned the city and salted the earth.

8.5.1 *Collapse of the Republic* (146-30 B.C.E.)

Rome's expansion from a small, inconsequential city on the Tiber River to a world state brought with it a profound and permanent change in Roman life. Wealth flowed into Rome from Spain after the Second Punic War. Simultaneously, Rome profited from the Greek influence that poured into Italy from the East. The traditional agrarian basis of Roman life was disrupted. Slavery increased and many small farmers lost their land to the growing *latifundia* (large, fortified estates owned by the aristocracy). Cato the Elder spoke for the conservative faction of the Senate when he warned that contact with Greek culture was eroding traditional Roman values. Between 146 and 30 B.C.E., a variety of political remedies were proposed. Ultimately, the Roman Republic proved unable to meet the challenges it faced.

8.5.2 The Gracchi Brothers

Tiberius Gracchi (163-133 B.C.E.) and his brother Gaius (153-121 B.C.E.) led a party (Populares or People's Party) that proposed a radical reform of the Roman Constitution. A powerful group of Senators, the Optimates (best men), opposed reform because they feared change would jeopardize their positions. The Gracchi brothers believed that the Republic's health was tied to the condition of the small farmers. Tiberius wanted to limit the amount of land that a Roman could own to 312 acres. Excess land would be distributed to the landless. Tiberius was assassinated (133 B.C.E.) before his reforms could be tested. Gaius continued his brother's efforts. He called for land reform and cheaper grain prices. Gaius enlisted the support of the Equestrians (former members of the Roman Cavalry). Many of the Equestrians were small businessmen who wanted to reform the Republic's finances. Battles between Gaius's supporters and opponents ensued. Gaius committed suicide in 121 B.C.E.

8.5.3 The Generals and the Republic

During the next eighty years power passed into the hands of military leaders. The Republic had outgrown its constitution. War broke out in Africa (Jugurthine War) and Italy was invaded by the Germanic tribes. The general Marius (157-86

B.C.E.), a "novus homa" (a new man or a person who was the first in his family to be elected consul) defeated Rome's external foes. Marius was less successful in stilling internal unrest. A revolt (The Social War) broke out in 90 B.C.E. Marius's successor, Sulla (138-78 B.C.E.), restored order by granting citizenship to those who could not meet the property qualifications. During the 70's and 60's Pompey and Caesar emerged as the most powerful men in the Republic. Manpower shortages had forced the Republic to depend on slave labor. In 73 B.C.E., Spartacus led a slave rebellion which the General Crassus suppressed. In the 60's Caesar helped suppress Cataline, who led a conspiracy in the Senate. In 60 B.C.E. Julius Caesar (100-44 B.C.E.) convinced Pompey (106-48 B.C.E.) and Crassus (d. 53 B.C.E.) to form the First Triumvirate. Crassus' death seven years later led to an open contest between Caesar and Pompey. In 49 B.C.E. Caesar crossed the Rubicon (the small river that separated his province from Italy). A civil war followed. In 47 B.C.E. the Senate proclaimed Caesar "dictator." Caesar gave himself the title of "imperator" (general). Two years later the Senate named him Consul for life. This led Brutus and Cassius to organize a conspiracy. The conspirators believed that Caesar had destroyed the Republic. In March 44 B.C.E. (the Ides of March), Caesar was assassinated at the Roman Forum. He died leaving his eighteen-year-old nephew and adopted son as his heir.

8.5.4 Caesar's Reforms

Under Caesar the Assembly possessed little power. He reformed the tax code and won popularity by easing the burdens of debtors. He ordered a commission to reform the calendar. The Julian calendar divided the year into 365 days with every fourth year having 366 days. This system was not revised until 1582 when Pope Gregory XIII introduced the current calendar.

8.6 CULTURE IN THE REPUBLIC

Until the end of the third century the Romans occupied themselves with tending their farms and making war. Carthage's defeat in the Second Punic War catalyzed an interest in Greek culture.

8.6.1 Literature and Philosophy

Platus (ca. 254-184 B.C.E.) adopted Greek Comedy to Roman circumstances. Terrence (ca. 190-159 B.C.E.) was a slave who wrote comedies in the tradition of Menander. Catullus (87-54 B.C.E.) was the most famous of the Roman lyric poets. Sallust (ca. 83-34 B.C.E.) won fame for his history of the Jugurthine War. The two dominant trends in Hellenistic philosophy, Epicureanism and Stoicism, found expression in Lucretius (ca. 94-54 B.C.E.) and Cicero (106-43 B.C.E.). Lucretius's *Order of Things* described the Epicurean atomic metaphysics while arguing against the idea of the soul's immortality. Cicero was the greatest orator and stylist in the Republic's last century. He defended the Stoic conception of natural law. His *Orations* present a detailed picture of Roman life at the end of the Republic. Cicero was assassinated by Mark Anthony's henchmen.

8.6.2 Religion

Rome's religious practices were influenced by both the Etruscans and the Greeks. The center of the Roman religion rested in the father (*paterfamilias*). The Roman religion's emphasis on civic-mindedness and patriotism contrasts with the Greek and Etruscan religions.

CHRONOLOGY OF THE ROMAN REPUBLIC

Expulsion of the Etruscan monarch,			
Founding of Roman Republic	509		B.C.E.
Law of Twelve Tables	449		
The end of the Struggle of the Orders	287		
First Punic War; Rome acquires provinces	264	-	241
Second Punic War; Hannibal is defeated	218	-	201
Third Punic War; destruction of Carthage	149	-	146
Land reforms by the Gracchi brothers;			
they are murdered by the Senate	133	-	122
Social War; Marius and Sulla struggle			
for power	90		
Slave revolt is led by Spartacus	73	-	71
First Triumvirate (Caesar, Pompey, Crassus)	60		
Caesar campaigns in Gaul	58	-	51
Caesar is dictator of Rome	49	-	44
Antony and Cleopatra are defeated at			
Actium by Octavian	31		

Etruscan Period: *She-Wolf*, **artist unknown, 500 B.C.E. Bronze. Capitoline Museum, Rome.**

CHAPTER 9

THE RISE AND FALL OF THE ROMAN EMPIRE

9.1 FOUNDATION OF THE EMPIRE (44-27 B.C.E.)

9.1.1 *End of the Republic*

Caesar's assassination produced a political vacuum. Many Senators hoped that the Senate would regain the prerogatives it had lost under the First Triumvirate (Pompey, Crassus, and Caesar). This was not to be the case. Caesar's Lieutenant, Mark Antony, led a powerful faction of Caesar's followers in Rome. Caesar's will confused the situation by naming Octavian (63 B.C.E. - 14 C.E.) his heir. Neither Antony nor Octavian had sufficient power to seize control of the state. Antony and Octavian invited Lepidus (governor of the western provinces) to form a Second Triumvirate which would "put the Republic in order" and punish Caesar's assassins. In 42 B.C.E., Brutus's and Cassius's armies were defeated at Philippi. The triumvirs divided the state. Lepidus gained Africa; Antony, Egypt and the east; and Octavian, Rome and the western provinces.

9.1.2 The Struggle for the Control of Rome (42-31 B.C.E.)

The conspirator's defeat removed the reason for cooperation between triumvirs. Lepidus soon lost his position. In 32 B.C.E., Octavian broke with Antony and war erupted. Octavian's forces defeated Antony and Cleopatra (Queen of Egypt in the Ptolemy Dynasty) at Actium (in western Greece) in 31 B.C.E. Antony and Cleopatra fled to Egypt where they committed suicide. At the age of thirty-two, Octavian had succeeded in making himself Rome's ruler.

9.1.3 Octavian's Governmental Reforms

Octavian wanted to avoid Caesar's fate. The secret of his success lay in his ability to maintain the outward forms of the republic while concentrating real power in himself. Instead of calling himself "imperator" (emperor), Octavian chose the title of "princeps" (first citizen). The reality was that all effective political and military power rested in him. In 27 B.C.E., Octavian consolidated his position. In a cleverly staged maneuver, he offered to relinquish his power. The Senate, swollen with Octavian's supporters, clamored for him to reconsider. The Senate handed him an overwhelming vote of confidence and a new title, "Augustus." In this way, Octavian secured a legal precedent for his autocratic ends.

9.1.4 The Principate of Augustus

Augustus ruled for forty-four years (31 B.C.E.-14 C.E.). The length of his reign was in itself an accomplishment after the decades of civil strife. Augustus introduced a number of important government reforms which won him popular support. These included a new system of coinage; new public services within Rome (police and fire protection); a new system of tax collection; and a policy which encouraged excess population to resettle in the provinces where they could receive farm land.

THE ROMAN EMPIRE (265 - 44 B.C.)

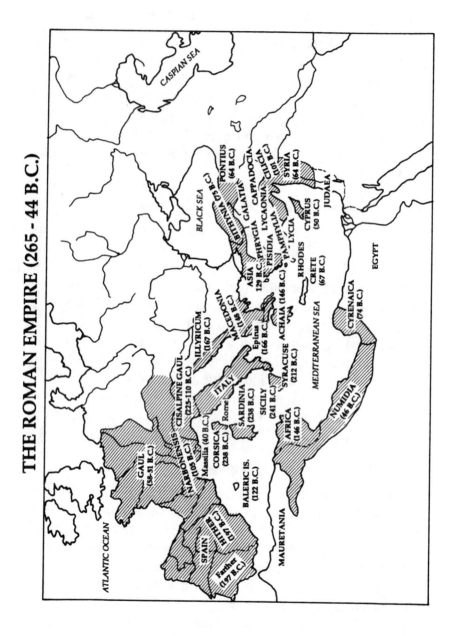

9.2 PAX ROMANA (27 B.C.E.-180 C.E.)

The first two centuries of the Roman Empire were a period of peace and prosperity. They are called the Pax Romana (Peace of Rome).

9.2.1 The Julian and Flavian Emperors

The four emperors that followed Augustus were either related to Augustus or to his third wife. They are called the Julio-Claudian Dynasty (14-60 C.E.) This line ended when Nero committed suicide in 68 C.E. A short, bloody civil war ensued with Vespasian emerging triumphant in 69 C.E. Vespasian's reign marked the beginning of the Flavian Dynasty which lasted until Nerva murdered Domitian in 96 C.E. During Vespasian's rule the Jews in Palestine revolted. Vespasian's forces defeated the rebels in 70 C.E. The Roman legionnaires destroyed the Temple in Jerusalem and dispersed the Jewish population. Pockets of Jews (Zealots) refused to concede defeat. In 73 C.E. a group of Jewish fighters chose to commit suicide rather than surrender their fortress at Masada on the west bank of the Dead Sea.

9.2.2 The Five Good Emperors

Despite the means that Nerva used to become Emperor, he is considered the first of the "Five Good Emperors" who governed the Empire between 96 and 180 C.E. Nerva introduced the tradition of the reigning emperor's naming his successor as his adopted son and heir. This insured a peaceful transition of power. The Five Good Emperors also included Trajan (98-117 C.E.); Hadrian (117-138 C.E.); Antoninus Pius (138-161 C.E.); and Marcus Aurelius (161-180 C.E.). Under Trajan the Empire grew to its largest size. Hadrian returned the Empire to the more defensible Augustan boundaries.

9.2.3 *Government and Society under the Pax Romana*

Economically, Rome flourished in the years between 14 and 180 C.E. The genius of the Augustan settlement lay in its success in enlisting the wealthy upper classes' support while simultaneously winning the approval of the masses. There are several reasons that account for this. First, the government possessed skillful and efficient administrators. Nerva introduced a system of public assistance (alimenta) to aid children without parents and other needy individuals. One problem that appeared under the Five Good Emperors and that was to grow in the third century was the beginning of a chronic labor shortage. Hadrian's retreat from the policy of expansion that had guided both the Republic and the early Empire had the unexpected effect of ending the flow of slaves from the newly conquered territories. Henceforth, the tenant farmer (colonus) became the basis of Roman agriculture. Trade expanded during this period as the Empire's fleet removed the threat of pirates from the Mediterranean. Roads were constructed that linked the most distant outposts with the capital. New cities were founded and the status of women and slaves improved. In the Republic, slaves received brutal treatment. Hadrian forbade the execution of slaves without a magistrate's approval. Women gained new rights. They could run businesses and make their own wills. Upper class women received educations that were much better than the Greeks had allowed their wives and daughters during the classical and Hellenistic Age.

9.3   CULTURE UNDER THE PAX ROMANA (27 B.C.E.–180 C.E.)

By the time of Caesar's assassination Rome had absorbed the main elements of Hellenism. Between 27 B.C.E. and 180 C.E., Roman culture achieved its highest accomplishments. The growth of Rome's cultural achievements paralleled the spread of Roman economic and political institutions. By 200 C.E. the

Mediterranean world and much of Europe and the Near East bore the unmistakable imprint of the Roman conception of literature, philosophy, science, and law.

9.3.1   *Literature in the Augustan Age* (27 B.C.E.–14 C.E.)

The period between 27 B.C.E. and 14 C.E. is called the Augustan Age. In these years Roman writers produced their greatest works. Vergil (70-19 B.C.E.). was the most important of the Augustan poets. In his *Ecologues* and *Bucolics* he proved his skill as a lyrical poet. The *Aeneid* was Vergil's greatest work. Commissioned by Augustus, the *Aeneid* presented Vergil's description of Rome's rise to greatness in epic form. Vergil's contemporary, Horace (65-8 B.C.E.), won fame as a lyric poet because of his *Odes*. Ovid (43 B.C.E.-18 C.E.) provoked Augustus into exiling him to Asia Minor when he published a poetical guide to seduction called the *Ars Amatoria*. Ovid's greatest work was his *Metamorphoses* in which he wove together a kind of history of Greek mythology. Livy (57 B.C.E.-17 C.E.) was the most famous historian of this period. Unlike Thucydides and Polybius, Livy did not draw on original sources. He patched his history together from earlier accounts. Livy's achievement was to create a narrative that traced the course of Rome's development from its earliest beginnings down to the Augustan Age.

9.3.2   *Literature in the Silver Age* (14-180 C.E.)

The period from Augustus's death until 180 C.E. is called the Silver Age. In general the writers during this period were less optimistic and hopeful than their predecessors. Seneca (5 B.C.E. to 65 C.E.) espoused Stoicism in his tragedies and satires. Juvenal (50-127 C.E.) was the most important first century satirist. Plutarch's (46-120 C.E.) *Parallel Lives* provided a portrait of Greek and Roman leaders while Tacitus (55-120 C.E.) criticized his era's weaknesses and follies in his histories.

9.3.3 Philosophy and Law in the Silver Age

Stoicism was the dominant philosophical movement during this period. Epictetus (ca. 60-120 C.E.), a slave, and the Emperor Marcus Aurelius (121-180 C.E.) were its chief exponents. They argued that virtue should be pursued for virtue's sake and strove to discover the natural laws which underpinned life. Rome made a unique and lasting contribution to western civilization in jurisprudence. The Roman's distinguished three orders of law: civil law (jus civile); law of the people (jus gentium); and natural law (jus naturale). Civil law applied to Rome's citizens; the law of the people merged Roman law with the legal percepts of the non-Roman peoples who formed part of the Empire; and finally, natural law consisted of principles that were discovered by reason and that bound all men together.

9.3.4 Science

The Romans were not theoreticians. Their strength in science lay in practical and applied science. Most of the contributions to science during this period came from individuals working in the Hellenistic tradition in the provinces. The Egyptian Ptolemy (second century) authored the thirteen volume *Almagest* which became the authoritative text for medieval astronomy. Ptolemy's contemporary, Galen (130-201 C.E.), conducted his medical research in Alexandria. The value of *Natural History*, Pliny the Elder's (23-79 C.E.) thirty-seven volume compilation of scientific lore, depended on the sources which he was using. Pliny's *History* was widely known in the Middle Ages.

9.3.5 Art and Architecture

Throughout the first two centuries of the Empire, Hellenism continued to be the main influence on Roman art and architecture. Rome's chief contribution was to increase the size of public undertakings. The Romans developed the use of concrete as a building material. The Flavian emperors ordered the construction of the Colosseum. The Pantheon (Temple to all Gods) was probably the most famous example of Roman architecture. Begun under Augustus and rebuilt under Hadrian, the Pantheon combined Greek architectural principles with the Roman style of construction on a grand scale.

9.3.6 Religion and Popular Entertainments

Roman culture in the first two centuries of the Common Era offers a paradox. While some Romans were advancing Hellenism and creating a rational conception of law based on Stoic principles, the masses were involved in popular entertainments and the cultivation of mystical religions. The gladiatorial contests of the Colosseum institutionalized the people's brutal appetite for fierce games. Simultaneously, mystery religions won large numbers of new converts. Isis (Egyptian fertility goddess) and Mithraism attracted a wide following. Followers of the god Mithra (whose birthday was celebrated on December 25), believed that Mithra had come to Earth to save man from evil. Those who believed in him would be rewarded with eternal life. There are parallels between Mithraism and early Christianity. The early Christians held a tremendous advantage over their rivals because of the Christians' willingness to include women in their religious observances. Some historians argue that the mystery religions were tied to the anxiety that grew after 180 C.E. The mystery religions offered a sedative to an increasingly unfriendly world.

9.4 THE CRISIS OF THE THIRD CENTURY

Marcus Aurelius's decision to name his son Commodus (reigned 180-192 C.E.) his successor proved the correctness of his predecessor's selection of those with talent rather than their own children as their heirs. After twelve years of vicious incompetence, Commodus was strangled by one of his followers. The next ten years saw three different emperors. In the third century Rome underwent both an internal and external crisis.

9.4.1 Society and the State in the Third Century

Civil war was nearly endemic in the third century. Between 235 and 284 C.E. there were 26 "barracks emperors." The consequences of the instability at the top of the Empire penetrated through the entire society. Economically, the Empire was unable to meet the costs of its defense. The government followed a policy of debasing coinage while placing a heavy tax burden on the population. These policies destroyed many small farmers and entrepreneurs, adding to the Empire's growing social problem.

9.4.2 The Barbarians

Rome's frontiers were threatened by barbarian invasion. In 224 C.E., a new Persian Dynasty, the Sassanians, attacked the Romans in Mesopotamia. In 260, the Sassanians managed to take the Emperor Valerian hostage. In the west and north, Rome faced the menace of the Germanic tribes. The Goths took the offensive in the 220's. By 250 C.E. they had captured Rome's Balkan provinces. In the fourth century the Huns erupted out of central Asia. Under the leadership of Attila they swept across Europe, driving the Visigoths and other Germanic tribes before them. In 378 the Visigoths defeated the Emperor Valens in the Battle of Andrianople. Thirty-two years later (410 C.E.) Alaric led the Visigoths as they looted Rome.

9.4.3 Culture in the Third Century

The literary and philosophic production of the third century reflected the climate of anxiety. Stoicism and Epicureanism continued to attract followers. Neoplatonism offered an alternative to the rational philosophical tradition. The Neoplatonist concentrated on the spiritual and mystical implications of Plato's philosophy. Plotinus (204-270 C.E.) was the founder of Neoplatonism. He argued that everything is an emanation of God. The World Soul is the first form of a continuous stream of God's emanations. Matter represents the final emanation. Each individual's soul is part of God. Plotinus believed that Neoplatonism offered the possibility of a mystical knowledge of God.

9.5 ROME'S DECLINE

9.5.1 *Diocletian and Constantine*

Diocletian (reigned 285-305) and Constantine (reigned 306-337) took drastic measures to stem the Empire's decline. Diocletian divided the Empire into four parts. Significantly, he moved his capital from the west to Nicomedia (a city in Asia Minor), and left the west under the control of one of his followers. Constantine followed Diocletian's lead, making his capital Constantinople.

9.5.2 *Causes for Rome's Fall*

A number of reasons for Rome's decline have been advanced. Some have argued that Rome's fall can be best explained as part of an overall moral crisis where Rome gradually lost its civic virtues and will to survive. Others have linked Rome's fall to the use of lead pipes in aqueducts and plumbing. Proponents of this theory claim that Rome's decline can be explained as the result of a general lead poisoning. Others have pointed out that the use of lead was too restricted to produce such a widespread effect. The eighteenth century historian, Edward Gibbon, argued that the rise of Christianity contributed to the Empire's decline. Christians were opposed to the values that were the basis of Roman society. Finally, there has been no shortage of accounts which identify the barbarian invasions

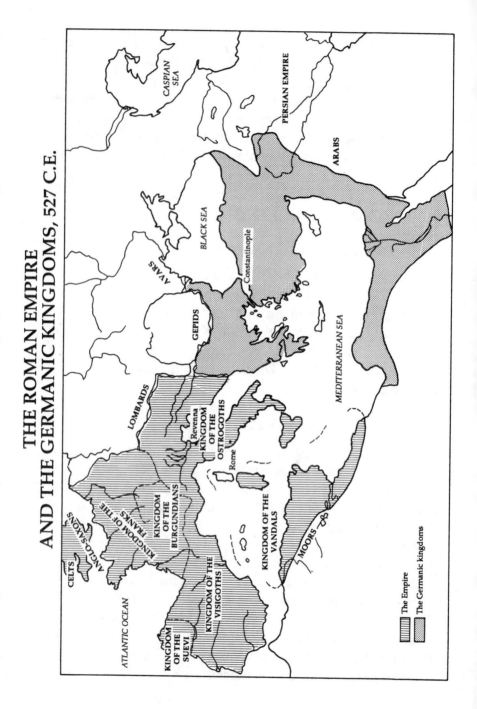

THE ROMAN EMPIRE
AND THE GERMANIC KINGDOMS, 527 C.E.

CASPIAN SEA

PERSIAN EMPIRE

ARABS

BLACK SEA

AVARS

Constantinople

GEPIDS

MEDITERRANEAN SEA

LOMBARDS

Revenna
KINGDOM
OF THE
OSTROGOTHS

Rome

KINGDOM OF THE
FRANKS

KINGDOM
OF THE
BURGUNDIANS

ANGLO-SAXONS

CELTS

ATLANTIC OCEAN

KINGDOM
OF THE
SUEVI

KINGDOM OF THE
VISIGOTHS

KINGDOM OF THE
VANDALS

MOORS

The Empire

The Germanic kingdoms

100

as the reason for Rome's fall.

9.5.3 *The Roman Accomplishment*

A number of recent historians have argued that the important question is not why Rome fell but rather why Rome endured as long as it did. Rome was the greatest empire in antiquity. It was an empire that was built on agriculture and conquest. It fell when the government and society were unable to provide a means of stable succession, develop an alternative to a slave economy, counter the widespread demoralization which showed itself in the lower birthrate from the third century forwards, and overcome the growing cynicism in the governing class. Nevertheless, Rome exerted a tremendous influence on subsequent generations. Rome supplied the framework for transmitting both Greek Culture and Christianity to the West.

CHRONOLOGY OF THE ROMAN EMPIRE

Octavian assumes the title Augustus and becomes, in effect, the first Roman emperor; start of pax Romana	27	B.C.E.
The death of Augustus; Tiberius gains the throne	14	C.E.
The Jewish revolt; Romans capture Jerusalem and destroy the second temple	66 -	70
Eruption of Mount Vesuvius and destruction of Pompeii and Herculaneum	79	
Hadrian crushes another revolt by the Hebrews	132 -	135
Marcus Aurelius dies; the end of the pax Romana	180	
Roman citizenship is granted to virtually all free inhabitants of Roman provinces	212	
Military anarchy; attacks by barbarians	235 -	285
Diocletian tries to deal with the crisis by creating a regimented state	285 -	305

Roman Empire: *Equestrian Statue of Marcus Aurelius,* **artist unknown, 80-161 C.E. Bronze. Piazza del Campidoglio, Rome.**

CHAPTER 10

CHRISTIANITY IN THE ANCIENT WORLD

10.1 THE ORIGINS OF CHRISTIANITY

The eventual triumph of Christianity over its rivals is partly explained by the religion's creed and the conditions present in the Roman Empire during the third and fourth centuries. Unlike the other mystery religions (chiefly Mithraism and Manichaeism), Christianity appealed to both men and women as well as across class lines. The unique appeal of Christianity, however, is inextricably linked to its founder's life and the work of Paul as his disciple.

10.1.1 *The Life of Jesus*

Jesus of Nazareth was born in Bethlehem around 4 B.C.E. (We owe the discrepancy of Jesus's birthdate to an error in calculation made by a sixth century monk.) When Jesus was thirty years old, John the Baptist (an ascetic evangelist) identified Jesus as "one mightier than I." During the next three years, Jesus ministered to the poor and sick. He preached a message of humility and brotherly love. His teachings eventually provoked the anger of the Pharisees, who considered Jesus's condemnation of pomp and ceremony a threat to their position. Jesus was brought before the Roman governor Pontius Pilate and accused of being a revolutionary. He was convicted and executed on the hill of Golgotha in Jerusalem. His followers despaired, fearing that Jesus's crucifixion meant the end of their master's religious movement. Then, a number of his followers reported that he had risen from the dead. Belief in Jesus's resurrection spread among his disciples.

10.1.2 *Jesus's Teachings*

There are no contemporary accounts of either Jesus's life or teachings. The Gospels (Good News) present the fullest record. The earliest of the Gospels (Mark), however, was written no earlier than 70 C.E. The Gospels of Matthew, Luke, and Mark are called synoptic because their authors based their narratives on a common text. The Gospel of John was the latest of the accounts and was written around 100 C.E. The Christian Scriptures consist of the Synoptic Gospels, the Gospel of John, the Acts of the Apostles, the 21 Epistles of Paul, and the Book of Revelations. There has never been an agreement among Christians as to the precise meaning of Jesus's message. Jesus preached a renunciation of the world and its temptations. He called on his followers to believe in him and dedicate their lives to faith, hope, and charity. The faithful would find forgiveness for their sins and salvation if they followed Jesus. They would be rewarded with everlasting life in heaven.

10.1.3 *Paul's Contribution to Christianity*

Saul of Tarus, or Paul (ca. 10-67 C.E.), transformed Christianity from a small sect of Jews who believed that Jesus was the Messiah into a world religion. Paul played a pivotal role in both the development of the Christian Church and the formulation of the religion's articles of faith. Paul was a Hellenized Jew who zealously supported the Pharisees. Around 35 C.E. Paul had a conversionary experience on the way to Damascus. Paul conceived of Christianity as a universal religion. Jesus's early followers considered Christianity a part of Judaism. James, Jesus's brother, led this faction in Jerusalem. He argued that Christians must be Jews and adhere to Jewish Law. Paul recognized that Christianity would be dealt a death blow if prospective converts must undergo circumcision before becoming Christian. Paul became the apostle to the gentiles. Eventually, Paul won out against his conservative fellow Christians. Paul's second contribution to Christianity came in his work as a missionary. He believed that all Christians were obligated to spread the Master's teachings (evangelist means "messenger").

10.1.4 *The Legacy of the First Christians*

Jesus's disciples believed in the imminent return of their Lord. Since the Kingdom of God was at hand, they were unconcerned with establishing an institutional base for Christianity. Paul changed this. Paul conceived of Christianity as a religion of personal salvation. His Epistles (letters to Christian communities) laid the basis for the religion's organization and sacraments (from the Latin "sacramentum," meaning oath or solemn obligation).

10.2 THE APPEAL OF CHRISTIANITY

Christianity's popularity during the first three centuries of the Common Era rested on several factors. First, Christianity's emotionalism and mysticism offered an alternative to the rational Hellenistic philosophical tradition. Second, the Pax Romana (27 B.C.E.-180 C.E.) allowed the early Christians to move freely throughout the Empire. The existence of a common language (koine) of trade, a Greek dialect, helped the Christian

PAUL'S MISSIONARY JOURNEYS

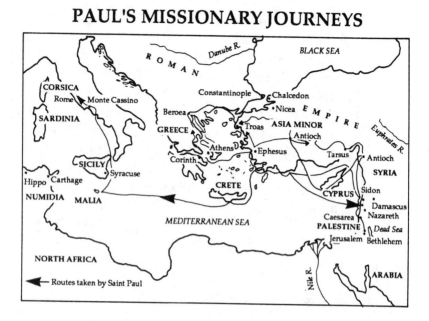

communities stay in contact with one another. Third, the internal and external threats that Rome experienced in the third century (Age of Anxiety) left many Romans in a state of confusion and alienation. Christianity offered solace to individuals who felt isolated in a harsh and troubling world.

10.2.1 *The Spread of Christianity Under the Roman Empire*

By the end of the first century Christianity had spread across the Roman Empire. During the second century Christian communities were firmly established. In the third century Christianity continued to grow despite sporadic official persecution. Finally, in the fourth century Christianity became Rome's official religion and the state began to persecute pagans.

SPREADING CHRISTIANITY

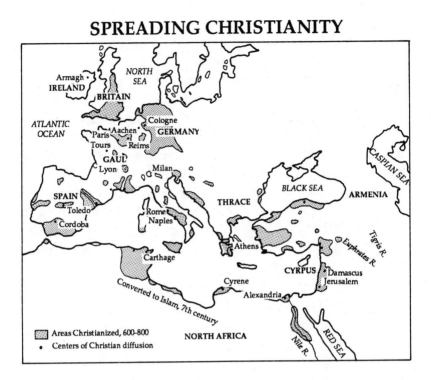

10.2.2 *The Persecution of Christianity Under the Empire*

The persecution of Christians under the Roman Empire was neither as extensive nor severe as once imagined. Generally, the Romans tolerated different religious beliefs. The official and popular hostility to the Christians can be divided into three categories. In the first century, there were sporadic attacks against the Christians. Officially, Nero took repressive steps against the Christians in 64 C.E. Most of the anti-Christian actions were, in fact, popular protests against the Christians' unwillingness to celebrate Roman holidays and acknowledge the state religion. In the third century, there were two periods of brutal persecution. The Emperors Decius (ca. 250 C.E.), Gallus (251-253 C.E.), and Valerian (253-260 C.E.) ordered the execution of many Christians. At the century's close, Diocletian

(284-305 C.E.) renewed the anti-Christian campaign. Under Diocletian the persecution reached its greatest extent. The next Emperor, Constantine, revoked the anti-Christian laws. Constantine converted to Christianity (ca. 312 C.E.) and ordered that the religion be tolerated in the Edict of Milan (ca. 313 C.E.). The evolution of Christianity from a persecuted sect reached its conclusion in 391 C.E. when Emperor Theodosius I (ca. 379-395 C.E.) proclaimed Christianity the Empire's official religion. Overall, the persecutions were neither extensive nor prolonged. The net effect may, in fact, have benefitted the early Christians in that the government's repressive measures and brutal actions strengthened the Christian community's faith and resolution.

10.2.3 *Formation of the Early Church*

The survival of Christianity in the first and second centuries depended on the success of the early Christians in creating an organization that would institutionalize Jesus and the Apostles' teachings while preventing the spread of heretical opinions. The first Christians practiced a baptism by water which served to remove original sin and a "love feast" (in Greek "agape"), followed by the eucharist (Greek thanksgiving, which commemorated the Master's Last Supper. Initially, the Christian communities had little organization. Groups of presbyters (elders) and deacons ("those who serve") gave guidance. Early in the second century, "episkopoi" (overseers) were elected by the congregations in different cities. The episkopoi or bishops governed the congregations and settled disputes. By the end of the second century, a clear hierarchy had developed. Bishops stood above priests. The Bishops of large cities were called metropolitans (today, archbishops). In the fourth century the Bishops who led the oldest and largest Christian cities (Rome, Jerusalem, Alexandria, Constantinople, and Antioch) were called patriarchs .

10.2.4 *The Rise of the Papacy*

During the early Roman Empire the Bishop of Rome had not yet achieved a position of supremacy over the other leaders of the church. Rome occupied a special place in Christianity because both Peter and Paul suffered martyrdom there. The Bishops of Rome pointed to the New Testament where Jesus told Peter that "on this rock I will build my church" ("Petra" in Greek means "rock"). Advocates of the Petrine claim that this passage should be interpreted to mean that Jesus chose Peter as his successor. Hence, the Bishop of Rome is the chosen head of the Catholic (universal) Christian church.

10.2.5 *Doctrinal Disputes*

In the first three centuries of the Christian epoch, disputes over the new religion's dogma posed a greater threat to the religion's survival than external persecution. Early in the fourth century, Bishop Arius of Alexandria (ca. 280-336 C.E.) argued that Jesus was a created being. This effectively eliminated the concept of the Trinity (God the Father, God the Son, and God the Holy Ghost). If Jesus was created, then he could not be of the same substance as God the Father. The advantage of Arius's doctrine (called the Arian Heresy) was that it offered a simple, rationalistic explanation of one of Christianity's enigmas. Bishop Athanasius of Alexandria (ca. 213-293 C.E.) opposed the Arianism. The dispute threatened to destroy the church. Constantine summoned the Christian bishops to the Council of Nicaea in 325 C.E. The Arian position was judged heretical and a statement of the articles of the Christian faith was proclaimed (Nicene Creed).

10.2.6 *Monasticism*

Constantine's conversion and the widespread acceptance of Christianity in the fourth century created problems as well as benefits. Many Christians feared that Christianity would be debased. These individuals sought ways to dedicate their lives to Jesus. In 320 C.E., Saint Pachomius founded the first monastery in Egypt. Saint Basil (ca. 329-379 C.E.) laid down the guidelines for eastern monasticism. Saint Benedict (ca. 480-543) created the pattern for western monasticism. Benedict's rule stipulated that monks must dedicate themselves to lives which combined work and prayer. The monastic day followed a fixed regimen from the day's opening prayer (before dawn) to vespers (evening prayer). Benedictine monasticism had at least three long-range effects. First, it expanded Christianity's influence among the barbarians through its missionary work; second, Benedict's rule lent a new emphasis to the importance of manual labor; and third, the Christian monasteries played an important role in the preservation of the classical Greek and Roman culture in their libraries.

10.3 THE EMERGENCE OF THE CHRISTIAN WORLD VIEW

Paul and the other Apostles established the foundations of Christianity. The early church fathers institutionalized these teachings in the early church. Tertullian (ca. 160-220 C.E.) attacked secular literature. He insisted that the Bible was all that any Christian needed, asking "What has Athens to do with Jerusalem?" In the fourth century Jerome, Ambrose, and Augustine provided the essentials of the Christian world view.

10.3.1 *Jerome* (ca. 340-420 C.E.)

Saint Jerome was an avid student of Greek and Latin literature. Fearing that his enthusiasm for pagan culture might endanger his immortal soul, Jerome retreated to a monastery outside of Bethlehem. There he produced his greatest work: a translation of the Hebrew Scriptures and Greek New Testament into Latin. Jerome's Bible (called the Vulgate) set the standard for Christianity in the west.

10.3.2 *Ambrose* (ca. 340-397 C.E.)

Ambrose was not a scholar. As archbishop of Milan, he was caught up in the day to day business of managing his diocese (from the Greek "dioikesis" meaning "housekeeping"). Ambrose found himself locked in a confrontation with Theodosius I because of the Emperor's massacre of innocent civilians. Ambrose successfully asserted the church's authority over a temporal leader and forced Theodosius to ask for forgiveness.

10.3.3 *Augustine* (354-430 C.E.)

Saint Augustine was born in North Africa. His father was a Manichaean while his mother (Monica) was a Christian. Augustine was raised a Manichaean over his mother's objections. (The Manichaeans believed there was a God of Good and a God of Evil who were at war.) Augustine studied rhetoric and moved to Rome and later to Milan where he taught rhetoric. When he was thirty-three, he converted to Christianity and was baptized by St. Ambrose. He became a priest and rose through the church's hierarchy until he returned to North Africa as the Bishop of Hippo. Augustine's two most important works were his *Confessions* and the *City of God*. In the *Confessions*, Augustine told the story of his struggle with evil and his final acceptance of Christ. In 410 C.E., the Visigoths sacked Rome. Many Christians despaired and questioned how God could allow such a misfortune to fall on his people. *The City of God* contains Augustine's answer to this question in the context of developing a Christian philosophy of history. Augustine argued that there is an earthly and a heavenly city: The City of Man and the City of God. All of man's pursuits are destined to fall into sin and corruption. The City of God is eternal. The Church is the sole means by which the chosen can pass from the City of Man to the City of God. Augustine made a radical break with the classical tradition. He based his interpretation on a concept of predestination and explicitly renounced the role of reason in the quest for salvation.

10.4 ROME'S DECLINE AND CHRISTIANITY

Rome did not collapse in a day. A number of factors account for the Empire's decline: soil exhaustion; manpower shortages; plagues; governmental incompetence; overtaxation; loss of civic virtue; the barbarian invasions; and Christianity. Rome did not cease to exist in 410 C.E. when Alaric led the Visigoths into the city. The Empire continued in the West until 476 C.E. (conventionally agreed on as the date of the western Empire's end) when Odoacer deposed Romulus Augustulus. The Roman Empire continued in the East (Byzantine Empire) nearly a thousand years longer until 1453 C.E. when the Turks captured Constantinople.

10.5 CHRISTIANITY AND THE CLASSICAL TRADITION

Christianity and the classical tradition represent two opposing currents in western civilization. The classical tradition emphasized the individual and the role of reason. Christianity demands that the faithful renounce worldly pursuits and acknowledge that man is fatally flawed. The early Christians simultaneously sought to refute and incorporate the Greek and Roman tradition. At the end of the fifth century the classical tradition stood in disarray. During the Middle Ages the Christian Church developed into the single most powerful institution in the east and west. The pagan tradition, however, was not dead. It would reawaken at the end of the medieval epoch in the Renaissance and the Age of Discovery.

CHRONOLOGY OF EARLY CHRISTIANITY

Jesus's crucifixion	29		C.E.
Saint Paul's missions	ca. 34	-	64
The Gospel According to Mark is written	ca. 66	-	70
The Gospel According to John is written	ca. 100		
A decade of brutal persecution of Christians by the Romans	250	-	260
Constantine grants toleration of Christianity/Edict of Milan	313		
The first convent is founded/Saint Pachomius	320		
The Council of Nicaea rules that God and Christ are of the same substance, coequal and coeternal	325		
Saint Jerome translates the Bible into Latin (the Vulgate)	340	-	420
Death of Saint Basil	379		
Theodosius I makes Christianity the state religion	392		
Death of Saint Augustine	430		
The Council of Chalcedon rules that Christ is truly God and truly man	451		
Monte Cassino is founded by Saint Benedict	529		

Interior, St. Paul Outside the Walls, Rome. **This prime example of an Early Christian basilica was begun in 386 C.E. Etching by G.B. Piranesi, 1749.**

"The ESSENTIALS" of HISTORY

REA's **Essentials of History** series offers a new approach to the study of history that is different from what has been available previously. Compared with conventional history outlines, the **Essentials of History** offer far more detail, with fuller explanations and interpretations of historical events and developments. Compared with voluminous historical tomes and textbooks, the **Essentials of History** offer a far more concise, less ponderous overview of each of the periods they cover.

The **Essentials of History** provide quick access to needed information, and will serve as handy reference sources at all times. The **Essentials of History** are prepared with REA's customary concern for high professional quality and student needs.

UNITED STATES HISTORY
1500 to 1789 From Colony to Republic
1789 to 1841 The Developing Nation
1841 to 1877 Westward Expansion & the Civil War
1877 to 1912 Industrialism, Foreign Expansion & the Progressive Era
1912 to 1941 World War I, the Depression & the New Deal
America since 1941: Emergence as a World Power

WORLD HISTORY
Ancient History (4500 BC to AD 500) The Emergence of Western Civilization
Medieval History (AD 500 to 1450) The Middle Ages

EUROPEAN HISTORY
1450 to 1648 The Renaissance, Reformation & Wars of Religion
1648 to 1789 Bourbon, Baroque & the Enlightenment
1789 to 1848 Revolution & the New European Order
1848 to 1914 Realism & Materialism
1914 to 1935 World War I & Europe in Crisis
Europe since 1935: From World War II to the Demise of Communism

CANADIAN HISTORY
Pre-Colonization to 1867
The Beginning of a Nation
1867 to Present
The Post-Confederate Nation

If you would like more information about any of these books,
complete the coupon below and return it to us or visit your local bookstore.

RESEARCH & EDUCATION ASSOCIATION
61 Ethel Road W. • Piscataway, New Jersey 08854
Phone: (732) 819-8880

Please send me more information about your History Essentials books

Name _____

Address _____

City _____ State _____ Zip _____
